S0-ASJ-638

Advance Praise for
"No, It's Not Hot In Here"
A Husband's Guide to Understanding Menopause

"This is the book I have wanted for years. I hope every meno-pausal woman buys at least one copy for her sweetheart. And men—don't think menopause won't affect you. If you live with or love any woman under the age of sixty, menopause will change your relationship. The advice and information is kind, loving, and superbly helpful. I smiled, cried, laughed and found myself in every page. This is a 'must-have' book."
> **Susun S. Weed**
> Author, *Menopausal Years: The Wise Woman Way*

"At last, a guide for men about menopause that answers their biggest question: 'What can I do to help?'"
> **Susan M. Love, M.D.**
> Author, *Dr. Susan Love's Hormone Book*

"This is a very informative, insightful read, but what pro-foundly touched me about this book was its sincerity and depth of caring. If every husband would only love his wife this much."
> **Dr. Stephen R. Covey**
> Author, *The Seven Habits of Highly Effective People*

"This is a great book! Dick Roth has taken one of life's signifi-cant challenges and turned it into a great growing and relationship-building experience. The content is thorough, readable, and helpful. But even more important, Dick's exam-ple of seeking to genuinely understand his partner teaches a process that can empower couples to solve this or any other challenge in life."
> **Roger and Rebecca Merrill**
> Authors, *First Things First* and *The Nature of Leadership*

"In an engaging expository and conversational style, Roth tells us everything we need to know without bogging down in polysyllabic scientific stuff or psychobabble. I highly recommend this book not only to husbands but also to wives, partners, and friends."

> **James A. Autry**
> **Author, *Confessions of an Accidental Businessman***

"When you read *'No, It's Not Hot In Here,'* you will be filled with gratitude to Dick Roth! We needed a menopause guide by and for men, and Dick has filled the vacuum with wisdom, clarity, sensitivity, and humor. Don't miss this great little book; it will make you smile and bring you closer."

> **Susan Page**
> **Author, *The Eight Essential Traits of Couples Who Thrive***

"Extremely well researched, an excellent resource for anyone, man or woman, dealing with the many issues of menopause. It gives a good synopsis of the physiology, psychology, pharmacology, and mythology of menopause. Strong work."

> **Bill Affolter, M.D.**

". . . an enjoyable and educational read. I found myself more than once thinking, 'Why didn't I already know that?' . . . an insightful and caring common man's analysis of the menopause process."

> **Steve Clark**
> **Legal Counsel**
> **Gold Medalist, 1964 Olympics**

"Dick Roth has written a book that I have long looked for to recommend for my patients on the topic of menopause. *'No, It's Not Hot In Here'* is accurate, informative, humorous, and a must for everyone in their midlife phase. It's not just for men, but for women as well."

H. Thompson Mann, M.D.
Gold Medalist, 1964 Olympics

"Roth has given couples a much-needed gift: a way for husbands to understand their spouse's menopause. I highly recommend this clear and concise guide."

John Gray, Ph.D.
Author, *Men Are From Mars, Women Are From Venus*

"Sensitive, caring, and wise. In addition to understanding the woman in your life, you will learn a lot about your own changes and how you and your partner can find common ground as friends and lovers. I wish I had read it when my wife was first going through the change."

Jed Diamond, L.C.S.W.
Author, *Male Menopause*

"With pristine clarity, an enjoyable sense of humor, terrific information with excellent references, and a compassion born out of direct experience, *'No, It's Not Hot In Here'* is very, very highly recommended—a Must Read for both men and women."

W. Brugh Joy, M.D., F.A.C.P.
Author, *Avalanche* and *Joy's Way*

"Dick Roth and I kept a childhood promise to each other . . . to win an Olympic Gold Medal in swimming during the 1964 Tokyo Olympics. As young teenagers, we held the world records in the 400-meter individual medley and were both expected to win. . . . To cope with the pressure of expectation, Dick and I would motivate each other by making bets such as, if you break a world record I will too; if you will win, I will win—however I could never have imagined the lengths (no pun intended) to which Dick Roth would go to keep a promise.

"Olympic record books rarely mention the fact that hours before Dick's Olympic final, he came down with acute appendicitis. Doctors warned him of dire consequences if he refused an immediate operation but he chose to risk everything rather than forgo a chance at winning an Olympic Gold Medal. His ability to handle pressure and pain inspired me to make good on our promise. I will always treasure my relationship with Dick, especially because we shared something that all should experience . . . friendship and support while in the pursuit of excellence.

"It is no wonder Dick has taken on another task of monumental proportions in writing a book about menopause. It is an honest and intimate account of his and his wife's journey through the emotional and frustrating minefield of myths, misconceptions, and research on a subject few want to deal with or acknowledge. Couples in menopause should read this book. It's full of answers, feelings, and common sense."

Donna E. de Varona
Chair, Organizing Committee, Woman's
  World Cup Soccer
Former ABC Executive and Emmy
  Award Winning Broadcaster
Two times Olympic Gold Medalist,
  Tokyo 1964

"No, It's Not Hot In Here"

"No, It's Not Hot In Here"

A Husband's Guide to Understanding Menopause

PUBLIC LIBRARY NEW LONDON, CT

Dick Roth

ANT HILL PRESS
Georgetown, Massachusetts

618.1
R

Copyright © 1999 Dick Roth

All rights reserved. No part of this book may be reproduced
by any means or in any form whatsoever without written
permission from the publisher, except for brief quotations
embodied in literary articles or reviews.

For permissions and reprint information,
contact Ant Hill Press:

Ant Hill Press
P.O. Box 10
Georgetown, MA 01833
(978) 352-9976
Fax: (978) 352-5586

1st Printing – Jan 99
2nd Printing – Feb 99

Printed in Canada
Webcom Limited – Toronto

ISBN 0-9655067-3-8

Edited by Sonia Nordenson
Cover design by Jeanne Marie White
Text design and composition by Jenna Dixon

Publisher's Cataloging-in-Publication
Roth, Dick (Richard William), 1947–
    No, it's not hot in here : a husband's guide to understand-
    ing menopause / by Dick Roth. — 1st ed.
    p.   cm.
Includes bibliographic references and index.
ISBN: 0-9655067-3-8
    1. Menopause—Popular works. I. Title.
RG186.R68   1999   612.6'65
                                        QBI98-1462

For Susan, the most courageous person I have ever known

Contents

La donna è mobile
Qual piuma al vento
(Woman is as changeable
as a feather in the wind)
—from the opera *Rigoletto,* words by
F. M. Piave, music by Giuseppe Verdi

Piave's wife may well have been going through menopause when he wrote these famous words. As Dick Roth explains (and thousands of generations of men have observed), during menopause some women seem incredibly and almost instantaneously changeable. Fortunately, Mr. Roth has taken the time to investigate and understand the myriad changes that occur to women's bodies, minds, and even spirits during menopause, and then has taken the time to share his understanding with us.

Remember when your daughter (or sister) went through puberty, especially the early years? Remember the mood shifts and changes—happiness one day, withdrawal and seeming depression the next, with no obvious explanation? Menopause is similar to puberty, with a "reverse twist": instead of increasing, hormones are declining.

During puberty, a young woman's hormones are coming on in "fits and starts," working their way towards a relatively steady adult pattern. Her brain cells are being increasingly but variably exposed to "adult" hormones that haven't been there in any appreciable quantities before. Those same hormones are causing remarkable bodily changes. And it's all happening whether she wants it to or not . . . no wonder a girl who's becoming a woman is such an unpredictable creature!

In a way, menopause is the reverse of this process. Instead of the (usually) steady, predictable monthly hormone cycle to which

ix

a woman has become accustomed, her adult hormones that increased so dramatically during puberty start "slipping and sliding" away, sometimes faster, sometimes slower. Her brain cells function with a "normal" quantity of hormones one day, and then try to function in the same way with considerably less hormones the next. Her body goes through changes as well . . . and she has no control over the process. No wonder a woman going through menopause can be so unpredictable!

As we men all "know," our hormones are more steady and predictable. We're not subject to monthly variability; we can count on our moods to fluctuate less. We don't have a menopause when our hormones decline very significantly in just a few years (or so we think . . . see Chapter Eleven). Since such a relatively abrupt menopause doesn't happen to us, it can be difficult to understand why the woman we thought we knew is suddenly behaving so strangely.

We're fortunate that Dick Roth is the man who's written this book for us. He has not only experienced his wife's menopause from a husband's point of view, but he's also an excellent writer, giving us complete but concise explanations of menopausal changes, in very understandable terms. He emphasizes the psychological as well as the physical aspects of a woman's transition through menopause. He suggests many ways to make the transition not only bearable, but a learning and growing experience for both partners.

In many ways, the generation presently entering menopause has shifted the emphasis from "She's pregnant" toward "We're pregnant." With Dick Roth's help, we can shift "She's going through menopause" more toward "We're going through menopause." Both these shifts in attitude will significantly strengthen a marriage and the bond of emotional partnership between a man and a woman.

— Jonathan V. Wright, M.D.
Medical Director, Tahoma Clinic, Kent, Washington
Co-Author, *Natural Hormone Replacement for
    Women over 45* (1997)
Natural Treatments for Male Menopause
    (December 1998)

Foreword

Dick Roth asked me to write this foreword because he wanted a "regular doctor" to introduce the book. As a regular doctor—a family practitioner, to be exact—I can tell you that you are about to read a very thorough, thoughtful, and well-balanced commentary on menopause.

Trust me, it is wonderful that you care and will spend some time trying to understand what your female partner is experiencing (or has experienced, or will experience). I am thrilled that you care and want to understand.

On a daily basis, for more than six and a half years in family practice, I have been trying to answer my patients' questions about female menopause. Some examples include: "What is menopause?" "How will I know when I have menopause?" "Is (fill in the blank with a symptom) part of menopause?" "Do I need hormone therapy?" "What other options are out there?"

Boy, do I get tired of hearing these same questions every day. In fact, my "regular doctor" advice is to stop right here. I mean it: stop reading this foreword right now! Proceed to reading this book—for the reason(s) that you picked it up.

For a long time, I have had only Gail Sheehy's book to recommend. Now Dick Roth's book can join Sheehy's as a useful resource for couples with questions about menopause. What I have to say about this book is relatively irrelevant. What you learn from this book is very relevant.

Why are you still reading this foreword? Turn the page, already.

— Pamela Farmer, M.D.

xi

"No, It's Not Hot In Here"

*I*ntroduction

Even after I finally accepted that my wife was going through menopause, I was still mystified. It all seemed new to me. She'd get bright red in the face and tear off layers of clothing at odd times, day and night. Some days she'd have no energy; on others, she could get so intense so quickly. I could never quite figure out what kind of mood she was in.

I really wanted to know what was going on.

I looked through her books about menopause, and even bought some more. But they were all missing something: advice for *me*. I kept looking for a book with a subtitle like *A Husband's Guide*. . . . I couldn't find one, and yet I knew that there are many other bewildered baby boomer husbands like me. And so the idea for this book was born.

Eventually I came to understand what was going on inside my wife, but to do this I had to sort through a lot of details—most of which I really didn't need to know. One of my objectives in writing this book is to give you enough information to inform you without overwhelming you. I think I've done enough sorting to give you a basic understanding of menopause. But if not, throughout these chapters and in the Resources section, I offer further references for those of you who want more detailed information on menopause.

My Terminology

I have wrestled with the question of what terminology to use in this book to describe the men and women who might read it. I know that you, my readers, may be men or women, husbands, boyfriends, significant others, even siblings or friends. Your "partners" will not all be "wives." But for simplicity's sake, I've chosen to make general use of the term "wife" to describe your significant other. And when I use pronouns like "you" and "we," I'm basically referring to men, even though some readers are bound to be women.

First and Foremost

One thing you need to know right up front is that, while every woman goes through menopause, *each woman's menopause is different.*

As an effect of her changing hormones, your wife may experience huge physical and emotional changes. Or she may barely notice anything. There are millions of women on both ends of the spectrum. Perhaps 5 to 10 percent sail right through menopause in a year, hardly aware of any effects; another 10 to 15 percent are deeply challenged—in some cases, for as long as a decade.

The vast majority of women are somewhere in the middle: affected, but not incapacitated, for a couple of years or so. They'll experience some, but not all, of menopause's physical and emotional signs. And they'll feel them to widely varying degrees.

Throughout this book, I'll be describing the most common effects of menopause. But remember that your wife will probably feel only a fraction of these.

What This Book Is About

Here's what I hope to include in this book: the information about menopause that women feel it's most relevant for their partners to know. Most often, women have told me that they simply want their husbands to understand what menopause is and isn't, and what they're experiencing. Women also want their partners to know that, when they have hot flashes or get emotional, they're not doing it on purpose, and that they're trying to learn how to respond to the imperatives of menopause as best they can.

I'll also do my best to address what men tell me they most need to understand:

- "How long will menopause last?"
- "What's it going to be like?"
- "How come my wife gets so emotional?"
- "Will she go crazy?"
- "How will this affect our sex life?"

Although this book won't be like going to school, you will get a little history, a little biology, a little psychology, and, if all goes well, a whole lot of common sense—all in an effort to help you and the woman in your life move gracefully through the transition called menopause.

We'll look first at the physical and psychological changes your wife may be going through. Then we'll examine the hard choices and controversies that she faces. You'll also hear about the advice your wife is likely to be getting, and about when, where, and how you can help her to assess this advice.

The menopause books I've read and the experts I've talked to are informative, to be sure, but often they've had conflicting points of view. I have had to work hard to distance myself from their sometimes strident and emotional arguments, in order to develop a relatively objective viewpoint.

During my process of gaining understanding, my own precon-
ceived notions—my ideas about whether women should take
supplemental hormones, for example—have been challenged
and sometimes changed. I truly hope I have gained enough
objectivity to present you with a balanced view of the various
positions and arguments regarding menopause. I suggest that
you do your best to try to suspend judgment until you understand not only the overview and details offered in this book,
but also how your wife, specifically, is affected by menopause.

It would be all too easy to stand back, point a finger at your
wife, and blame her menopause for any relationship problems.
As another option, some men try avoidance, with remedies like
young blonds, red Corvettes, and the Hair Club. But neither
blame nor avoidance really works. Instead, we'll take a more
commonsense approach by examining menopause as an opportunity to strengthen a relationship through developing understanding, empathy, patience, and love.

There is no doubt that menopause offers a woman's soul a
chance to grow. Much has been written about using this transition as a passage into a rich and fulfilling next chapter of life.
We'll look at how women can make the most of this trying but
promising time in their lives.

And let us not forget that men's souls have an opportunity to
grow as well—and not just because of a midlife crisis. We'll take
a look at how we can make the most of our own passage into
the wisdom years of our lives.

Though I'll be advising you to add to your own understanding,
the menopause transition is not just about men learning to listen,
adjust, and be tolerant. True, many women are already good at
relationship-building skills, and many men must work to get themselves into an equally understanding mode. Yet I'm not suggest-
ing that men do most of the work—even though, in many cases,
they may have to work hard to become more compassionate.

Relationships are always two-sided. I will definitely not be
advising men merely to shut up, stuff their feelings, and let
their menopausal partners have their way. In any relationship,

both people need to listen well and to speak honestly and considerately.

A Personal Note and an Invitation

While my wife's menopause has not been easy, I wouldn't trade these past few years for anything. Nothing, outside of parenthood, has offered us so much opportunity to deepen our relationship through communication and mutual appreciation.

My menopausal learning curve started with me at ground zero, clueless. If my wife's menopause had offered me just the opportunity to communicate and learn, I would be grateful. Yet not only have I gained understanding of what was going on inside my wife (and, as it turned out, inside of me), but I've also been able to learn something about acceptance.

So often I haven't wanted to accept what life has to offer me. It's not just aging. I don't especially like the struggles, disappointments, humblings, and other so-called negative experiences of life, either. During my wife's menopausal transition, though, I've learned to value the process of accepting life's gifts, however daunting they may appear. Sometimes I have struggled with myself and my weaknesses. It was hard to realize that my youth was not eternal. Yet more than once I've been grateful to have been humbled as I've learned how to respond more gracefully to the ups and downs of life and marriage.

As I get older, life keeps offering me opportunities to give, to grow, and to become a better human being—one not so caught up in his own self-centered desires. I have come to accept and even to appreciate the wisdom that may be gained through welcoming life's changes.

I want to invite you to not fear menopause, but to see it for what it is: a transition from one stage of life to another. I hope that you, too, will learn and grow as you understand and help your wife. And I hope that your relationship, like my wife's and mine, will deepen and become richer.

As you make your own midlife transition, I also want to invite you to look for your own opportunities to grow. The chance to come closer to what will truly fulfill you and make you happy is a wonderful gift. Your midlife years represent a unique threshold. You can hang back, holding on to the imperatives of your past—your conquests, accomplishments, and acquisitions—or step into a life filled with the joys of expanding your involvement beyond yourself. You can cling to your passing youth, or keep moving forward to find completely new adventures.

1

"What Is Going On with My Wife?"

As Butch Cassidy said to the Sundance Kid, "Every day we get older. Now that's a law." Most of us don't want to grow old. We do what we can to cover up any signs of age. We dye our hair, dress like twenty-year-olds, or do radical comb-overs. But, like the man said, aging is a law.

For every woman, part of getting older is the arrival of menopause. No exceptions. It's natural—happens to every woman on Earth. And if you're a husband, menopause will play a part in your relationship.

The Choice Between Resistance and Understanding

Most men don't want to know about menopause. We go into denial about it and try to ignore it. But since you're reading this, I'm assuming that something has broken through your resistance. You care. You want to know what your wife is experiencing and how you can help.

The greatest help you can give your wife is to understand what she's going through. There's really nothing you can do to change or fix things; her body is going to do what it will. She has some choices in the process, but whether or not menopause happens is not one of them. She can only choose how she is going to respond.

You have some choices, too. But they are only about how you can respond to what's happening inside her. Your first job is to understand. Through that increased understanding, you can become supportive.

The New Awareness

The present wave of menopause awareness is new, and our baby boomer wives are driving it. This is the same generation of women who pioneered the return to natural childbirth. I'll bet your father didn't go to a Lamaze class or coach your mother's breathing during labor. And he sure wasn't allowed in a birthing room. But you were.

It has only been in our lifetimes that menopause has even been talked about in "polite society." I know your dad didn't read a book about it. And I'll bet he never talked to your mom about it, either.

Not too long ago, many women going through "the change" were diagnosed with dementia and locked up as if there were something wrong with them. It wasn't until the early 1990s, when the leading edge of the baby boomers began to have hot flashes, that the current wave of popular books on "the pause" started to appear in bookstores and women began to openly discuss the subject. But the menopause of our own wife still sneaks up on most of us husbands.

Cycles, Yes. But Menopause?

It used to be that every twenty-eight days, give or take a day or two, my wife got her period. The calendar would get marked with a telltale dot, and we could reliably count the days to the next arrival.

If she was emotional and I couldn't figure out why, I'd sneak off to the calendar, find the last dot, and count twenty-eight days. About three days before the upcoming event, I could expect that she'd be tired, edgy, maybe cranky or depressed, and sometimes insecure.

I gradually learned that I couldn't do anything to change her cycles and emotions, but I sure could do something about how I responded to them. If I answered her crankiness with anger, I risked making a hurtful argument out of what would have quickly faded away. But whenever I managed to avoid making the moment more intense with my own reactions, her emotions passed easily. Over time and through much trial and error, I found out that it was wise to be accepting instead of reactive.

What helped me the most was simply understanding what was going on inside her. I eventually developed an ability to step back a little and watch as the monthly tides swept over her. Whenever I could separate myself from the process, I saw that these monthly cycles are something larger than my wife, something that all women are subject to.

In time, I developed a kind of awe toward these forces. I saw that my wife's natural cycles are an essential part of preserving the species so life can go on. If the human race is to reproduce, periods are going to happen.

Then, just when I was getting used to it all, it changed.

On my wife's fortieth birthday, she got a period that lasted almost two weeks. It was so unusual that she scheduled one of her infrequent visits to a gynecologist.

She came home with some unexpected news: the doctor had told her that she was in the beginning stages of premenopause and that her irregularity was normal.

You couldn't have shocked me more. My wife menopausal? No way. Menopause was something I associated with our mothers' generation. Susan was way too young. I thought about her shriveling up, getting saggy breasts, and growing a hump in her back—and promptly went into denial. I married a young, slim, sexy woman. She's not growing old. Nope. No way. Uh-uh.

"Old" Doesn't Mean "Useless"

I've come to understand that my denial, while it may have some deep psychological causes, is pretty easy to explain. Our society has scripted us in countless ways to believe that "old" equals "used up" and "useless." From Hollywood to Madison Avenue, from the drug companies to the medical community, from the fitness industry to the New Agers, we are taught in a thousand subtle ways that youth is desirable and old is a disease, that wrinkles are wretched, that baldness is bad, and that gray needs to be covered up.

This is particularly true with regard to menopause. In many countries and societies—Japan, for instance—there is very little psychological trauma associated with this transition. It's expected and accepted. In other cultures, like those of the Native Americans, it's even honored as an entrance to a life of wisdom.

But in the United States, menopause is seen as a medical condition.

Menopause Is Not an Illness

Until the 1950s and 1960s, our society often treated menopausal women as hysterical. Doctors even gave women shock treatments to get them over it. Then the medical community saw that menopause has a biological basis, so surgeons treated it by removing the offending organ. Even today, the operation to remove a woman's uterus is called a hysterectomy. An appendectomy takes out an appendix; a hysterectomy is supposed to take out hysterics.

Small wonder that women and their husbands don't want to face menopause.

While the shock treatments and hysterectomy options are still resorted to today, they began losing ground to drugs and then to hormones. In the 1960s we tranquilized women with Valium and Librium. That option soon fell out of favor, because these drugs don't work on menopause and they do create addictions.

Since then doctors have been prescribing hormones. The very fact that hormones are prescribed by doctors for the "symptoms" of menopause reveals our cultural mindset. We have come to believe that menopause is an illness, with symptoms that need to be treated by a doctor.

How can something that every woman goes through be a disease? That notion has to be terribly degrading to a woman. Having a disease means something is wrong with you. If menopause is a disease, that means there's something wrong with every woman. Only a man could have thought that one up. (His name is Robert Wilson—more about him later.)

• • •

No wonder I didn't want to accept that my wife was going through menopause. Besides my own fears and prejudices about aging, I had the societally conditioned idea that this would mean there was something wrong with her. Maybe it would mean trips to doctors and hospitals, or to psychiatrists and institutions.

I may have been firmly in denial, but my wife pressed on with my education. She told me that the doctor had said her "symptoms" would continue, but that it would probably be years before real menopause happened. Yet I didn't hear much that Susan said; I still couldn't even associate the word "menopause" with my young and beautiful wife.

Some Terminology of Menopause

Before we go any further, let's get our terminology straight. This is a book written by a husband, for other husbands. It's not for doctors and professionals (though it has been reviewed by them for accuracy). It's for regular guys who want to understand and support their wives and partners through a potentially difficult time. So I will use everyday language instead of the sometimes confusing medical terms.

The confusion starts with the term "premenopause" or "*peri*-menopause," which technically refers to the prolonged transitional time span, typically two years or more, that leads up to a woman's final period or "menopause" (a "pause" of the menses). Some authorities say that a woman officially enters menopause the day her last period ends. Others say that menopause begins one year from the day her last period began.

The confusion continues with the term "*post*menopause," which is sometimes used to describe the time from the last period to the end of hot flashes. It is also used to describe the time after all the signs of menopause have stopped. "The climacteric" is the medical term for the whole pre- and post-menopausal time period, which can range in duration from a year to a decade or more but typically lasts only a few years.

But you won't hear too many men saying "My wife's going through the climacteric." We more commonly toss out something like "I think my wife must be in menopause," to mean that she's having hot flashes and seems to have eternal PMS. Since the term "menopause" is the one most commonly used to describe the whole process, that's the one I'll chiefly use in this book.

Premenopause

The time leading up to menopause is always unique. There are some relatively common signs of its approach, like irregular periods and the first warm flushes, but the timing, the duration, and the intensity of premenopause are impossible to predict. Your story may be like mine, or it may be different. Regardless, you'll probably see some similarities.

• • •

My wife's occasional irregular periods really didn't cause me too much concern. They just meant a brief glitch in my ability to time her PMS. But everything was still regular enough for me to remain blissfully in denial.

After a couple of years, though, she completely missed a period. She had been late before, but unless she was pregnant, her periods had always arrived. Another kid was not in our plans, so we were worried about the lapse.

Off to the drugstore I went for an early-pregnancy test kit. After some anxious moments, the results were negative. Just to be sure, we did the test over again. Not pregnant. We breathed a shared sigh of relief.

The next period came right on the dot. *Hey,* I thought, *anybody could miss one. No big deal.*

Then, a year or so later, it happened again. And again Susan wasn't pregnant. Then came months more of the old regularity. It went on like this for a while: every so often within her otherwise regular cycles, she would skip a period.

Then the whole thing began to change. My wife's monthly blood flow started to vary; some periods were heavier, some were prolonged, and a few were still regular, coming at twenty-eight days. Some periods took as long as three cycles to appear. These made her really uncomfortable; she felt on the verge of getting her period for three months. She'd be bloated, sore, and emotional, just like PMS, but she'd never get the relief of having her menstrual flow come.

The irregularity affected Susan's emotional peaks and valleys, too. Her cycles were so unpredictable that I couldn't time her PMS.

I was now in a bit of a bind. I'd become able to accept a certain amount of my wife's emotions simply because I knew they would pass in a few days. If I didn't get defensive, things would mellow out. But, with her new irregularity, I didn't know which surges were temporary and which weren't, which were directed at me and which were just blowing off steam.

In typically male fashion, I reacted defensively to them all . . . which didn't help our relationship.

So Let's Fix It

I tried discussing the changes with my wife, but I hadn't yet developed any of the patience and openness that can help so much. Like many men, I tend to look at things as if every effect has an immediate cause. If there's something wrong, just take a couple of steps back, see what's causing it, and fix it.

I used to do this with my wife's problems. I'd analyze them and get them all figured out, as if I knew what was going on inside of her. Then I'd make a wise pronouncement.

She'd get a little touchy when I pulled something like: "About to get your period, huh? That's why you're uptight. All you need to do is let it go. Next time you feel this way, just check the calendar, count the days, and cut me a little slack."

But now I couldn't rely on my old form of boneheadedness. I was getting into even deeper trouble.

Actually, Susan and I could talk about what was happening to her physically—big blood flows, extended periods, no periods, and so forth. But the emotional swings were increasingly mysterious to me. I couldn't figure out what to do about them, or how to bring them up without making matters worse.

These irregular cycles continued off and on for years. Sometimes she'd get her period right on time for months, and sometimes she'd miss one or two or three, or be a couple of weeks late, or get one right after another, or have one that lasted for almost two weeks. We never knew what to expect. But we got used to it. And in my denial I tried not to give another thought to menopause.

Flashing

It was sometime during this period that Susan first started asking me if it was hot in the house or if I'd turned up the heater (it eventually got to be a joke between us; that's where the title of this book came from). These are classic signs of the first "warm flushes." The warm spells weren't too noticeable—nothing like the volcanic action that was to come. They kind of sneaked up on her, lasted a few minutes, and went away. My wife would just be warm at funny times. I didn't think much of it, because it wasn't too disturbing.

But when the hot flashes started in earnest, they got my attention. There was no way not to notice them. They were intense, disruptive, and powerful, and they could happen anywhere. All of a sudden, layers of clothes would come peeling off and anything handy could become a fan. Susan would tie up her hair, get red in the face, and stop whatever she was doing.

When they happened at night, she'd wake up boiling hot, toss off the covers, take off her nightgown, and open the windows. Then, as quickly as the flash had come, it would be gone. She'd be all wet and cold. The clothes and covers would go back on, or in the most extreme cases would get changed because they were too damp. The windows would be closed, and Susan would eventually let out a great sigh of relief.

It was intense.

At first the hot flashes came infrequently, but at their peak they built up to several an hour. It was back to the doctors. Suspecting menopause, they took her blood, measured her estrogen, and told her that her hormone levels were normal. So, the doctor said, even though she'd missed months worth of periods, she wasn't menopausal.

What Could It Be?

If this wasn't menopause, I wondered, then what was going on?

Now, because of a confusion in terms, I was totally in the dark. Maybe "technically" my wife wasn't menopausal, since her periods hadn't stopped and the tests said her hormone levels were normal. But, in the vernacular, she was "in menopause." I was clueless and confused.

When Susan first got pregnant, she made a point, like so many women of our generation, of learning about what was happening inside her. She read books, talked to friends, and became an aware and informed participant. She went to Lamaze classes, got me to be a helper, and then had both our children naturally.

So, even though the doctor had totally confused us with the terminology about her blood test results, my wife went ahead and learned about menopause anyway, mostly through books and talking to her sister and friends—doing her best to figure it all out.

• • •

Eventually I followed suit. The first thing I came to understand is how amazing a woman's body is. It has all these hormones and cycles, and it has organs that can grow and nourish a baby. In the next chapter, we'll look at what happens inside a woman's body that begins with her first period and ends with menopause.

$2\mathcal{T}$he Marvel of a Woman's Body

The female body has to be one of the most impressive creations in nature. The more I've learned about women and menopause, the more I stand in awe of what it takes for us to reproduce ourselves. The workings of the female body inspire me. It's the very dance of creation, a waltz of wonderment. Biologically, women are impossibly complex. Their chemistry is as subtle as a delicately flavored gourmet soup, only a hundred times more intricate.

Amazing Womankind

Briefly, here's what happens inside a woman that enables our species to live on. This is also what stops happening at menopause.

Once a month, with uncanny regularity, an inborn message triggers a change in the balance of chemical messengers in a woman's veins, and her blood washes her cells with an ages-old reproductive call. In response, new micromixes of hormones go into action, some commanding other hormone-producing organs, some turning cellular functions on and off like a light, and some acting as direct agents, causing her reproductive tissues to swell.

No one knows precisely what initiates this innate life-sustaining process. We can be taught to point to a woman's glands, organs, and portions of the brain, like the pituitary, the ovaries, and the hypothalamus, and to say where this or that hormone is produced or received.

We can learn long lists of confusing scientific names and initials, like estrodial, estrone, and progesterone, or LH, FSH, and GnRH. We can measure her hormones, time them, replace them, and observe their actions. We can try to understand the process, or even try to control it.

But the more we come to know about a woman's inborn reproductive system, the more we must stand in awe.

In the amazing monthly cycle that enables a woman to reproduce humankind, all of her three trillion cells are flushed with her hormonal messengers, but only a relative handful, a billion or so in her ovaries, are stimulated into action. After these ovarian cells receive the signals that only they are equipped to receive, they grow toward their unique purpose: to ready this month's single egg for a possible mating with one of a man's three hundred million frantically competing sperm cells, swimming for their lives in a do-or-die race.

Of course, the mating is only a possibility. Regardless, a woman's body goes through the ritual every twenty-eight days or so, in an unfailing attempt to be prepared.

Ovaries, Ova, and Ovulation

Nature, in her wisdom, has provided every woman with more than enough eggs to ensure the continuation of our species—way more than she'll ever use. But all she'll ever have.

As a female grew in her own mother's womb, her cells differentiated differently from those of a male, creating ovaries, a uterus, and a vagina instead of a scrotum, testes, and a penis. By the time of her birth, her ovaries contained as many as half a million single-celled eggs, repositories of her genetic contribution to evolution.

From the onset of her menstruation, or menarche (from the

Greek words meaning "month" and "beginning"), at about age twelve or thirteen, to her last period or menopause (also from the Greek, meaning "month" and "cessation") at around fifty, a woman's ovaries prepare her eggs in their follicles. They start with about four or five hundred thousand eggs, and prepare as many as one thousand per month, or ten thousand to twelve thousand per year. The ovaries might prepare fewer and fewer eggs with the passing of time, but the body keeps on preparing ova to start new life until the supply is gone.

Monthly, as a woman's system is stimulated by her hormones, between a dozen and a thousand of these eggs begin to grow inside her ovaries, swelling in their protective coverings, known as follicles. Almost always, only one matures enough to disgorge an egg; the rest wither and die. These follicles turn out to be of great importance, because along with the egg they release estrogen and progesterone, the female hormones that are of such concern during menopause.

During the human female's four decades of fertility, each of her two ovaries, while at rest, is about the size and shape of an almond in its shell, but quite smooth-surfaced, as if the almond were shelled and peeled. When stimulated, the growing ovarian follicles swell up like a cluster of soap bubbles. What was once small, smooth, and regular grows large, lumpy, and asymmetrical as several follicles compete for the chance to be the only one to release an egg, or ovum.

Nobody really knows why one follicle prevails, but when a woman's body has, in its wisdom, chosen from among the candidates, that one continues to expand, balloon-like, until there is an enormous bulging on the ovary's surface. At its fullest point, the ripe follicle bursts and casts the mature ovum toward the fallopian tube and the swimming sperm, in the phenomenon known as ovulation.

Along with the egg, the follicle releases a wash of hormones that trigger the body to create a place in the uterus to nurture the fertilized egg. After a few days, if no sperm is successful in its quest and the egg is not fertilized, the uterus somehow knows, and other homones are released that in turn trigger both the unfertilized egg and the uterine lining to be sloughed as menstrual flow.

And then the cycle starts all over again.

Hormones

However, if a single sperm cell had succeeded in penetrating the egg, the fertilized ovum would then have sent a different set of hormonal signals through the blood, and the woman's body would have engaged in an entirely different process. In this case, if all goes as planned, the fertilized egg attaches to the lining of the uterus, finds nourishment, divides, differentiates, grows, and—perhaps, if everything goes well—becomes another new human being.

Either way it goes, period or pregnancy, the process is determined by changes in the delicate internal balance of hormones. A small change in one hormone level and follicle growth is stimulated; a few micrograms of another—far less than half a grain of salt—and the uterus begins making ready to receive the ovum.

• • •

Whether or not we know them by name, we men know about hormones; we feel their effects in our own bodies. Just a small increase in testosterone might make us aggressive, sexual, or even violent. The bodies of men and women alike make this "male hormone," but men create eight or ten times more of it than women do. Likewise, male bodies manufacture the "female hormones" estrogen and progesterone, but in far smaller batches than female bodies do.

While the amounts of hormones produced by men and women are different, the major difference lies in how they are released into our systems over time. Men get a huge rush of attention-getting testosterone in puberty, but other than that we go through life on a pretty direct hormonal course, plodding forward step by step. After our awakening surge, our daily production of testosterone slowly and inexorably shrinks as we get older. The level ebbs gradually enough that we usually don't notice our diminished capacity until we get into our forties or fifties.

• • •

By contrast, our female partners hormonally surge and flow like waves within the larger tides, feeling rushes monthly. The content of their blood is constantly being balanced and rebalanced by their reproductive imperatives.

As women's levels of estrogen and other hormones ebb and flow cyclically, all kinds of effects, both physical and emotional, are created. Estrogen alone affects more than three hundred of a woman's bodily functions. It does everything from lubricating her skin to regulating her internal thermostat.

Instinctual Cycles

Men can never really know what a woman's cycles feel like. We can get some idea by observing our own hormonal changes, but it's not really the same. And since very little research has been done on male testosterone levels, we have only our own feelings to go on if we want to try to understand our wives' cycles.

The closest you'll get to knowing what your wife goes through is to watch the rising and falling of your own sexual desire. I am assuming that most of you reading this are in your forties and fifties and, like me, will soon be experiencing a diminishing of your sexual drive. As you get older and the fires are somewhat abated, if you stop and look, you can notice peaks and valleys. You won't feel anything close to the intensity of your wife's monthly surges, but you can get perhaps a glimmering of an understanding of how much her feelings,

desires, urges, and impulses are affected by the cyclical barrage of hormones.

You might notice in yourself how there's a sort of primal, ani-
mal force that comes unbidden, causing thoughts of sex to rise
seemingly on their own. It doesn't do any good to ignore these
thoughts—that won't make them go away. If you don't exercise
control, these thoughts can start to affect your behavior. Unfulfilled, they can affect your moods. At times a certain member of
your body seems to have a mind of its own, rising toward its
appointed duty without a thought from you.

These urges are a force of nature. They happen to you. It's
part of putting on a human body. Without the use of self-aware-
ness, self-control, and the application of your will, you are at
this instinctual force's mercy.

In its naturalness, what you feel as sexuality is similar to what
women go through monthly, though it's by no means the same
in complexity or intensity. You just feel amorous, deal with it
however you do, and go on. Think about it: sexual urges just
come upon you, and to some degree they govern you. At best,
you can only change how you respond to their promptings.

The End of a Phase

Women can't keep their periods or menopause from happening, either.

Long before a woman's final period, her egg production
starts to get irregular. At some point, when the supply is
becoming depleted, the follicles may no longer grow and
release an egg with its corresponding bath of hormones. In
other words, she skips a period.

The female body compensates for the lack of estrogen in a
variety of ways, first by overcompensating and putting out
more hormones in an attempt to stimulate those follicles to
grow. Sometimes it works, and the remaining follicles swell
again and succeed in casting another egg toward the uterus.

Thus, the first outward sign that menopause is approaching is a missed or irregular period or two. Usually this happens long before we suspect, or want to suspect, menopause. When our partner first misses a period, most of us (like me) just pass it off and forget about it. This premenopausal phase may begin for some women in their early forties or even their thirties, while other women may not miss a period until their early fifties.

Some scientists think the decrease in egg production happens because the ovaries get scarred from all the follicle eruptions and have a harder time swelling and releasing an egg through all the scar tissue. Others think the decrease is due to having fewer fertile follicles left to work with. What matters is not so much why it happens but that it happens: when the eggs start to run out, the periods begin to stop, and hormone production changes.

• • •

Besides irregular periods, the ebb and compensatory overflow of estrogen and other hormones can trigger intense reactions in a woman that we've come to recognize as the common signs of menopause. The next two chapters will give you a thumbnail sketch of how these signs might appear in your wife.

3 Physical Changes

M aybe the only fact about menopause that's universal is that each woman's is unique. We can talk about the average age that menopause begins or what it's typically like, but you can't tell from these averages what will happen to your wife. One way to figure out what her menopause might be like is to check how it was with her mother, but even within families there can be wide differences.

So, as you read about some typical signs and manifestations of this universal female passage, please remember that *each woman's menopause is different.*

Physical Changes That Will Go Away

The most noticeable changes that come to a woman's body during menopause will go away, usually within just a very few years. Unless your partner is one of the really rare ones, her hot flashes, night sweats, and itchy skin will be gone pretty quickly. It doesn't mean they won't bother her; they probably will. It doesn't mean you can ignore them; the menopausal signs will have their effects. But it does mean that there's light at the end of the tunnel.

Hot Flashes

If your wife is one of the 85 to 90 percent of women who have hot flashes, these heat rushes will probably be the first things she notices besides missing a period. These annoying internal saunas are part of a large group of effects that doctors think result from lower levels of estrogen in her blood, which begin when one of her follicles doesn't release an egg.

About half of the women who have hot flashes report that the disturbances last about a year; a third say they last for two or three years. Most of the rest of menopausal women are done with them in five years, but a small percentage have hot flashes for life.

Here are a couple of typical descriptions:

- "It's hard to describe. This hot feeling starts inside, around my neck, and comes out. I can't control it; it's like the flu or a fever. Sometimes it's like a slow burn, sometimes more like a volcano. It just spreads out from the inside."

- "They start with a feeling of anxiety. Then the heat starts coming from the inside—from my center, my core—and spreads out. It gets hotter and hotter until it breaks. It seems like it affects my whole body, and my face gets bright red. It's very uncomfortable. If you could will them to come when it was cold it would be really great. But no . . . They come when they want to."

These rushes can range from barely noticeable to overwhelming, can last for just a few minutes or as long as an hour, and can happen anywhere from a few times to more than fifty times a day.

While a woman's internal temperature actually remains pretty constant during a hot flash, her skin temperature can rise as much as *six or eight degrees in two or three minutes.* Clearly, this is more than enough to make her tear off her clothing, throw open windows, and perspire profusely.

When she starts cooling off, the perspiration chills her and her skin temperature actually drops a degree or two below where she started. Sweaters go back on, windows close, and heaters get turned up.

This much internal combustion is an energy drain. Flashes can be irritating, even humiliating. A woman might get one during a meeting at work and turn bright red and start to perspire. The intense ones will distract her or make her really uncomfortable. She'll probably have to get up and leave the meeting to fan herself and cool off, and may even have to change her blouse.

Since hot flashes often begin with a rush of anxiety, they can trigger uneasiness, worry, and angst. This nonspecific anxiety can shoot holes in a woman's confidence, and this can be especially true if she's in an environment that isn't supportive. It would be great if she could control the timing of her flashes and schedule them for lunchtime or breaks, but she can't.

There's a lot of speculation about what brings on a hot flash, and not a lot of agreement. Some say it's a hot room; some think it's stress; others say it's the time of day; some think it's sex; some say it's elements in the diet, especially alcohol or caffeine; and others believe it's psychological.

It doesn't really matter what brings one on. What's important is how you respond to your wife when they happen. You need to understand that she's uncomfortable, she's not doing it on purpose, and there's nothing she can do to stop it. But at least it'll pass, and usually in just a few minutes.

There's universal agreement that hot flashes can't be willed away or brought under control with a positive attitude. Hormone replacement therapy (HRT), which we will talk about later in detail, is usually effective in reducing or eliminating hot flashes. It seems that, since hot flashes are linked to a reduction in estrogen, adding estrogen makes them go away. Not everything is yet known about the biology of hot flashes though, because some women's flashes will go away by using natural progesterone instead of supplemental estrogen (a potentially important distinction—more on this later).

Night Sweats

Hot flashes don't quit while a woman sleeps; they're just called by a different name: night sweats. Mild ones wake her up. Medium ones might get her up for a nightgown change. My wife's were so intense that she would occasionally drench the sheets enough to need to change them.

While not really different from a daytime hot flash, night sweats have even more bothersome effects, and not just on nightgowns and sheets. Because a woman is asleep when her temperature rises, she can't adjust her layers as she warms up. The result is that she wakes up in a full sweat. Worst of all, night sweats can interrupt her sleep over and over again in the course of a single night.

One woman described them this way: "At the peak of my hot flashes, I'd have five or six big ones a night. I'd wake up all worried, then I'd realize I was flashing. When they first started, I'd just soak the sheets and we'd have to change them, but later I would get up and go into the bathroom to wait one out. That way my husband wouldn't have to get up. But still I'd have to change my nightgown and I'd be awake for an hour."

The worst part of getting night sweats can be the exhaustion. Imagine if you were awakened every couple of hours all night long, every night for years. And then you were kept awake and uncomfortable for a while. Then you still had to get up every morning to go to your job.

Here's what another woman says: "It's like having a newborn, but the night awakenings last for years, not months. And they aren't a source of joy, just fatigue. And it all happens when you're not so young any more, but middle-aged!"

The effects of sleep deprivation can be so extensive that some books maintain that menopause's moods are completely caused by lack of sleep. That idea sounds extreme to me, but it seems pretty reasonable that getting so tired from so many night sweats might add to the intensity of whatever a woman is feeling. At the very least, exhaustion can make her worries worse—and might make her irritated or short with her spouse.

Another effect that many experts attribute to night sweats is short-term memory loss, as in "Have you seen my car keys?" With so little sleep, some women can get too tired to concentrate. They may think less clearly for a while, or be less able to follow a detailed conversation, or they may even seem irrational.

You probably would too, if you were that exhausted.

Some women are able to overcome this fuzzy thinking by sheer force of will, and can still concentrate at a high level all day long. But after a full day at work, a woman may need to let down. In other words, she might keep track of her responsibilities all day long but lose her keys the minute she gets home.

Psychologists say that disturbed sleep not only makes us tired, it also upsets the psyche by keeping us from dreaming. They tell us that we need that deep REM sleep to stay psychologically balanced.

So it's pretty safe to assume that night sweats will have more effects than causing a woman to buy an extra couple of nightgowns.

Heart Palpitations

A "heart flash" can come right on top of a hot flash, or it can come on its own. One woman described them this way: "When I had my first one, I thought I was having a heart attack or something. I was working in the garden and my heart just took off. All I could do was lie down and listen to it. It was just beating so hard, it freaked me out. But it went away pretty fast."

While disturbing and worrisome—the heart might beat wildly at up to two hundred beats per minute—these heart palpitations are apparently not physically harmful. But the effect on you and your wife can be wild, causing panicky trips to the doctor or even the emergency room.

Not much is known about these palpitations. Not nearly as many women get them as get hot flashes. Stress, heat, and exertion are some of the things that can trigger them. If your wife gets these heart rushes as a result of menopause, they tend to go away about the same time that her hot flashes do. Needless to say, though, something this intense should not be ignored. You should suggest, as with anything that appears this serious, that your wife ask a doctor about her heart flashes.

Nausea

As if all of the above were not enough, menopause can also bring on attacks of nausea. These attacks can range from mild, quickly passing discomfort to fainting, vomiting, diarrhea, breathing troubles, and exhaustion. If any of this happens, you probably won't have to suggest to your wife that she check with a doctor. The trouble is, though, that since these symptoms can point to any of numerous disorders, misdiagnosis is common.

A Myriad More

Another prickly bother to quite a few menopausal women is a tingling of the skin. My wife describes it this way: "It's like there are ants crawling across my forehead. Sometimes I catch myself brushing them off as if they're really there."

Nobody knows what brings this on; though annoying, it's apparently harmless. Doctors call it formication. Maybe it's ants making love.

Other physical effects that a woman might experience are migraine headaches; flaky fingernails; itchy or painful joints; fuzzy peripheral vision; hair that's more prone to breakage; and sore, aching muscles, particularly in her neck and back. Most of these can be traced to either her hormone levels or the way her blood flows through her vessels. Fortunately, they're temporary; they go away with the passing of menopause.

The whole thing sounds pretty disruptive and challenging, doesn't it? But remember, your wife will probably experience only a fraction of the above.

Physical Changes That Won't Go Away

A different group of changes are more lasting, profound, and universal. But they are normal, a part of almost everybody's aging process—both genders. We all need to pay attention. These changes include brittle bones, heart disease, wrinkled skin, and a diminished sex drive.

Men usually age gradually. If you are a man, your skin will wrinkle over decades; your hair thins all your life; your muscles and bones lose their strength little by little; and your sex drive slowly lessens. But in some cases, the quick drop in a woman's estrogen supply can make these changes seem more pronounced in her. Your wife can have all of these effects happen seemingly all at once, in the few years right around menopause. If this occurs, you'll probably notice the changes.

Either way, aging is natural. It's not to be ignored, but don't think that medicine can "cure" it, either.

Calcium Deficiency and Osteoporosis

An almost invisible change that is accelerated with menopause is how a woman's body turns calcium into bone.

All our lives, both men's and women's bones act as a calcium bank, releasing reserves when other parts of our system, such as our nerves and muscles, need some. Before about the age of thirty-five, our bones take in more calcium than is withdrawn, and the calcium level increases. After thirty-five, the process is reversed and the calcium level in our bones slowly decreases over the years.

When the decrease is severe, it's called osteoporosis. Bones may lose as much as 20 or 30 percent of their volume, and can become porous, brittle, and easily broken.

While every male and female body goes through the same process of bone absorption and thinning, for women, during the few years around menopause, the thinning process is significantly accelerated. The lower level of estrogen in a woman's blood causes her bones to temporarily lose some of their ability to absorb calcium. Thankfully, the rate of calcium loss will slow down after menopause.

If some precautions are not taken, women may be prone to broken bones later in their lives. Effective treatments are available, ranging from replacing the hormones to herbs, exercise, acupuncture, and calcium supplements.

There is no question that hormone replacement therapy (HRT) can slow the rate at which a woman's bones lose calcium. But there is a potential downside to hormone supplements, and whether or not to use HRT is likely to be one of your wife's toughest decisions. We'll discuss this issue in detail in Chapter Eight.

One direct drawback to taking hormones to counteract bone loss is that hormones will only postpone the loss. If a woman ever stops taking her estrogen, she'll lose as much bone as if she had never taken it at all.

The best cure for osteoporosis is prevention. Building strong bones before the age of thirty-five through good diet and lots of exercise is the surest way to avoid later bone loss. By now, your wife's bone density has pretty much been determined.

You probably should be talking to your daughter about osteoporosis. The time that she really needs the exercise and calcium is in the first half of her life. After I found out about this, I made sure my daughter had a supply of calcium supplements. After she read this chapter, I think she even started taking them, and I know she started exercising.

Genetics have a lot to do with a woman's susceptibility to osteoporosis. For Hispanic and African-American women, whose bones are about 10 to 20 percent more dense than those of their fairer-skinned cousins, the chances of getting osteoporosis are quite low. But about 25 percent of Asian and Caucasian women are subject to some pretty substantial bone thinning.

If your wife is fair-skinned and thin-boned, if she ever smoked cigarettes, or if her mother had osteoporosis, she'd better pay attention. For her, good dietary calcium, from milk, broccoli, and leafy green veggies, is a must, and so is vitamin D, from the sun. Weight-bearing exercise such as walking or low-impact aerobics is also universally recommended to keep the bones strong.

You can be a big help here by going on walks with your wife and trying to eat a good diet yourself. While you have less chance of getting osteoporosis because of your gender, exercise and good diet are good ideas anyway. And who knows? The walks could do a lot for your relationship.

Heart Disease

The older a woman is, the greater her chance of a heart attack. It has not been proven that this fact is related to menopause, but it seems likely. Earlier in life, strokes, heart attacks, clogged arteries, and high blood pressure favor men. Women are somehow protected.

We know that menopause doesn't directly cause heart failure; usually heart attacks happen because of clogged arteries. But the drop in estrogen is probably a contributor to heart disease. By age sixty-five, women's rate of heart disease starts to catch up with men's. By seventy-five, heart disease doesn't discriminate between genders. From then on it is the major cause of death in both sexes.

Cholesterol is the big heart health problem. You've heard it before: when we eat too much fatty food and don't get enough exercise, cholesterol gums up our arteries, making them smaller so less blood can flow. It would be like pouring roofing tar inside of a fire hose. Enough tar would make for less water flow. The pump would have to work harder to keep the water flowing, and would wear out sooner. A worn-out pump equals a heart attack.

In the prevention of osteoporosis, estrogen has been seen to directly affect calcium loss, yet it seems that the hormone might play only an indirect part in keeping a woman's heart healthy. The studies are still inconclusive, but they suggest that, by regulating both HDL and LDL (the "good" and "bad" kinds of cholesterol), supplemental estrogen helps lessen cholesterol buildup.

The mechanisms, causes, and processes that link estrogen and cholesterol are not yet fully understood. And, while estrogen supplementation may help a woman's heart health, it works in reverse in men. One study showed that men double their likelihood of a heart attack if they take estrogen.

We men need to be taking special care of our hearts, too—especially since at midlife and for the next couple of decades we are at much higher risk of a heart attack than our wives are. We all know what a healthy heart diet looks like: low fat, whole grains, leafy greens, and not too much meat. Include a baby aspirin, regular exercise, and a happy relationship and you have the whole prescription for good heart care.

You could serve as an example here. You know what I mean: cut down on the burgers, cut out the ice cream, ask for broccoli, take her for a walk instead of watching one more football game—that kind of thing.

Did I mention yet that those walks might do your relationship some good?

So why don't we do it? One reason might be that we don't have enough support to make it through all the temptations.

Did I say support?

Could you and your wife support each other?

Watch out. If you help each other through midlife and beyond, you just might find yourselves in a pretty good relationship.

Her Skin

One of the big fears men have about menopause it that it's going to turn that beautiful smooth-skinned woman undressing for bed into a wrinkled old "whatever."

There's no doubt that your wife is going to get wrinkles; so will you. Everybody does. Wrinkles come from time, from years of smiling and frowning, and from summers of catching rays.

A lack of estrogen doesn't cause wrinkles, and adding estrogen via HRT won't cure them. The government makes the drug companies write that right on the label. Estrogen may soften the wrinkling process by adding moisture under the skin. But regardless of what the cosmetic industry wants us to believe, nothing keeps wrinkles at bay forever; even a face-lift is only temporary.

We have all been unconsciously influenced by our culture to think that youth is good and aging is bad. A natural part of growing older is having an older-looking body. In a society obsessed with smooth skin and body-fat measurements, the desire to maintain a youthful-looking body has created whole industries.

Unfortunately, in my opinion.

Now, don't get me wrong, I think a healthy body is a good idea—a whole lot better than the alternative. But if we go so far as to attach our identity to a youthful body, where does that leave us when we get old?

Midlife and menopause offer both men and women a chance to look inside and develop ourselves into what we really are, which is much more than just a body. We are human beings with minds, hearts, and souls, and we have the potential to create and contribute based on our unique inner qualities of character, experience, and wisdom.

So I say that we should reframe the issue, and look upon wrinkles and aging as a good sign—a sign of deepening toward our inner selves.

• • •

There is one more physical change that may happen to your wife—one that deserves a chapter of its own. It has to do with sex.

4 *M*enopause and Sex

T here are a lot of misconceptions about sex and menopause. That's what makes it so interesting to find out the
truth.

The Big Myth

Like a lot of men, not only was I afraid that my wife would
shrivel up and go nuts during menopause, I also thought she'd
lose all interest in sex. I'm glad to say that none of the above
has happened.

While it is true that up to half of the women surveyed in the
various studies have said that they experienced a drop in their
sexual urges during menopause, *about a quarter have said that*
they felt an increase.

In almost all of the women who notice a decrease in their
sexual urges, the change is temporary. And the decrease is
nearly always brought on by physical discomfort like hot
flashes or exhaustion, not because a woman's sexual switch is
suddenly shut off.

It fascinates me that some women actually feel more sexual
during and after menopause. I've always assumed that women,
like men, experience a gradual decrease of sexuality, but apparently this isn't necessarily so. Many women report that not hav-

ing to worry about pregnancy enables them to enjoy sex more. Also, when a woman's level of estrogen drops with menopause it means she has proportionately more testosterone, the big sexual-urge hormone. Some experts figure that it is because women can feel their testosterone more that they actually are more sexual during and after menopause.

What Does Change

While her sexual *drive* is not necessarily affected, her sexual *organs* are. Again, every menopause is different; your wife will experience the following changes in her own unique way.

The Ovaries and Uterus

While a decrease in estrogen may or may not affect her sex drive, your wife's changing hormones will definitely and directly transform the systems that were designed to create and nurture new humans.

When a woman's ovaries have finished contributing their supply of eggs, her body gets the signal that its childbearing years are past. The organs that functioned to produce babies are not needed as before, and they take on new forms. The ovaries and uterus shrink, although, interestingly, they still produce valuable hormones—especially estrogen—but in smaller amounts now.

Doctors used to remove the uterus and ovaries as a matter of course. They figured that, since the organs weren't needed any more for childbearing, they should be taken out before they caused any trouble. Some doctors still do remove them, but thankfully we've come to recognize the postmenopausal importance of these organs. The automatic reflex to separate a woman from her uterus and ovaries is now not nearly so strong.

But so many hysterectomies are still being done on premenopausal women that menopause writers have taken to calling a normally occurring menopause "natural menopause." A "surgical menopause" is one that happens because a doctor has removed a woman's ovaries.

Hormones, Cycles, and Birth Control

It's important to remember that, during menopause, even as the ovaries and uterus are completing their function of preparing eggs, they are still contributing hormones. As I said before, a woman's periods often become irregular before they stop. In response to a missed period, hormonal levels can vary widely as the body attempts to restart the swelling of the eggs in their follicles.

The ovarian follicles, after they have released their eggs, are responsible for producing a uterus-nourishing bath of hormones. The body's attempts to rebalance the hormones can cause a woman's estrogen and progesterone cycles to fluctuate. The follicles might even respond with enough extra of these two powerful hormones, or enough shortfall of others, to cause the uterine lining to be retained for weeks or even months. That's why your wife might be bloated and feel as if she has eternal PMS, yet not get her period.

Then, after several months or even a year, the mix of hormones might finally trigger the uterus to let go of its lining, and your wife, with a great sigh of relief, might get a long overdue period. But even though the uterus held onto its lining, the ovaries might have gone on producing eggs while menstruation was suspended.

What this means is that, even if your wife might not have gotten her period for up to a year, she could still have been ovulating and fertile. For this reason, doctors usually advise a woman who uses birth control to keep on using it for a minimum of a year following her final period. Some doctors advise keeping up the birth control for as long as eighteen to twenty-four months.

But beware: if the only birth control you use is the rhythm method, it can't be trusted. The hormonal surges are not likely to follow any predictable pattern during the menopausal transition.

Recent studies have shown that many women continue in a somewhat irregular hormonal cycle for as long as five years after their last period. Although not producing eggs, the ovaries and uterus still produce estrogen and progesterone in fairly significant amounts. This has important consequences in two areas: first, because those hormones are important to a woman, care should be taken in considering whether a hysterectomy should be performed. And second, the fact that a woman still produces hormones is important in deciding how much hormone replacement she may need, if any.

The Breasts

A woman's breasts are also affected by menopause. When her hormonal changes signal that her breasts won't be used for feeding babies any more, the lactating cells and mammary glands are no longer rebuilt. These are the tissues that give the bosom firmness and support, so as a result a woman's post-menopausal breasts may sometimes lose their bulk and may also lose some altitude.

This might have unconscious effects on both you and your wife, and the only way I know to counter the unconscious is through awareness. It can really help you if you know this effect is coming and can prepare yourself for it. As with the skin, outer changes will happen. Again, we need to learn to identify with the deeper, more lasting parts of ourselves. If you can not only see but affirm your wife's inner worth and beauty, you can help her as well, because her changing body may be negatively affecting her self-image.

The Vagina

You really do need to be aware of this next physical effect.

When there is less estrogen in her bloodstream, a woman's vaginal walls often thin, and they can lose their elasticity.

Before menopause, the vagina secreted an abundance of fluids during foreplay that made penetration easier (this also made it easier for sperm to swim). When estrogen levels are lower, the vaginal tissues take longer to release fluid and may not release nearly as much.

If your wife's vagina is drier, sex can hurt her. She may need some help in the form of a lubricant, more prolonged stimulation, or slower penetration. Be considerate. Take your time. Think of *her.*

Doctors often prescribe different forms of estrogen to help with vaginal dryness. While we'll devote an entire chapter to the pros and cons of hormone replacements, this is one area of HRT that's definitely worth mentioning now.

Your wife will almost surely be advised by her doctor to use lubricants when she's having sex. She also may get a prescription for a vaginal hormone cream. *Be careful—these hormone creams are not lubricants. They should not be used when you're having sex, or at any time close to sex.*

Hormone creams are medications, normally applied daily at a time when sex is not expected. Estrogen creams are designed to bring readily absorbable estrogen directly to a site that will benefit from it. The hormones are absorbed into a woman's system through her vaginal tissue. Over time—weeks, or maybe even months—the estrogen reestablishes premenopausal moistness. If the hormone cream is present during sex, the estrogen will be absorbed into you as well. Not a good idea.

Stick to water-based lubricants. "When she's dry, try KY."

Fortunately for you maybe, some other advice your wife might be hearing about her vagina is to "use it or lose it." It seems that a woman will continue to secrete greater amounts of vaginal fluids if she is regularly aroused. Obviously, you can be a help here.

But be careful to heed your wife's moods and wishes. If she doesn't want to have sex at any given moment, it probably has more to do with the effects of menopause than with you—unless you've been so insensitive that you've turned her off.

It's Not You, It's Biology

We men tend to make lots of mistakes with regard to sex and menopause, mostly because of ignorance. As a husband, it's easy to assume the worst: that she won't ever want to have sex again, or that it's you she's lost interest in. But if a woman avoids sex, it's usually because of pain or exhaustion or hot flashes.

I know that many people have a tough time talking about sex, but when your wife is going through menopause it's a good idea. Find out what's up for her. Men often assume they know, but usually we don't have a clue. Try to understand before you jump to any conclusions. That's good generic advice that may have benefits way beyond your menopausal sex education.

When you add in everything else that a woman in midlife is going through, being romantic might sometimes be pretty far from her mind. I know it's hard, especially where sex is involved, but try not to take this personally.

One woman said it this way: " . . . And then there were all the hot flashes, too. It seemed like just when we were getting into it I'd go volcanic. But even more than that, sex hurt. I think he took it personally, but that wasn't it at all. It just hurt for him to be inside me. Would you please tell him that it isn't him? It's biology."

In preparing to write this book, I've asked a lot of women what they want from their husbands. Far and away, the number one answer is something like this: "Understanding. I just wish he could understand what I'm going through."

What About What's Happening to You?

Another thing about sex and midlife: you might be having problems of your own.

A woman's estrogen shuts off pretty quickly, but a man doesn't lose his testosterone all at once. If you're like me, that huge teenage spike of juice might have kept your mind on sex for years.

But all the while, your supply of testosterone has been slowly ebbing. Again if you're like me, you might have noticed some years back that you're not thinking about sex all the time any more, just every so often. What used to be constant is now cyclical and, maybe every once in a while, not totally over-whelming.

Doctors tell us that having less testosterone can make our erections softer and smaller and can occasionally even keep us from having an orgasm. To the man who has strongly defined himself by his virility, this can be disturbing, maybe even threatening.

If you have identified with your sexuality over the years, los-ing an erection can trigger some deep psychological reactions, like trying to compensate by demanding more sex or, worse yet, trying to prove you're still manly by getting it on with a young beauty. You know the archetype—the guy with a midlife crisis who leaves his wife, buys a Corvette, and runs off with a trophy blond. And it wouldn't be unlikely for that kind of man to blame his ex-wife for his actions.

Menopause is such a nice catch-all, so easy to blame things on. But blaming is a bad idea in any case, and especially so in menopause.

Less sexual energy on your part can be a real benefit if your wife is one of the women who want less sex during menopause. I know this may sound sacrilegious to the macho, but think of it—you might end up being on the same wavelength as your wife. And you might even be appreciated for it.

Many physical factors influence sexuality during menopause, but since half of all women feel like having sex as much or more during menopause, the half that feel less drive can't be "diag-nosed" with some universal physical problem. So what else might be influencing menopausal women?

• • •

This brings us to one of the most controversial areas of menopause writing and research: a woman's psychological and emotional changes. The next two chapters will attempt to unravel some of the confusion and controversy.

5 *T*he Many Moods of Menopause

S ome people maintain that menopause causes no emotional changes. On the other hand, there's a persistent myth that the typical menopausal woman goes nuts. You know: catatonic, incoherent, or just terminally cranky. As it happens, both of these assertions are untrue.

A menopausal woman might get anxious and worried, she'll almost certainly get tired, and she might get cranky from time to time. But there's no evidence that menopause will make her go off the deep end. There are very few areas of agreement among menopause experts, but this is one: *all* the studies have shown that *there is no rise in depression or serious mental illness because of menopause.*

But a lot of us husbands might say, "OK, sure, but what about when I just don't know what to expect? I mean, one minute she's her old self and the next, well . . . I just can't figure her out any more. *Something's* going on."

It's true—something is going on. In this chapter we will try to sort out what that something might be.

Controversy and Confusion

After I got the idea to write this book, I began to check out the menopause books that were already out there. I was amazed by different they are. Their perspectives range from the purely medical, at one end of the spectrum, to the highly feminist at the other. They can go from conservative to New Age; from traditional to spiritual; from angry to soothing; and from "take control of your life" to "accept what's happening to you."

The woman in your life may have gotten her first advice, and maybe her first book about menopause, from a friend. (My wife keeps a couple of copies of her favorite around, as loaners.) After she finishes that first book, don't be surprised if your wife goes to the bookstore to look for more. There, her choices are staggering.

At your local Barnes and Noble, she's likely to find more than fifty books on menopause at any one time. If your wife didn't get overwhelmed by the choices, she probably at least got confused. And she could easily have bought something on one end or the other of any of the controversies.

Being a male author, I am somewhat removed from the fray. While I'll state both sides of the argument just so you know what your wife might be hearing, I hope to represent the middle of the spectrum—where I think the best advice resides.

The Stereotypical Menopausal Woman, Hollywood Style

In a movie that came out a few years back, Michael Douglas plays an over-the-edge accounting nerd who snaps in a traffic jam and walks across L.A. to see his daughter, turning into Rambo and wreaking havoc along the way. Robert Duvall is the cop who is supposed to stop him.

In an unnecessary plot thickener, Duvall is only a couple of days from his retirement. As he chases down our nerdy Rambo, he also has to deal with his incoherent wife. She's anal, paranoid, overbearing, and a mess. Of course, the reason is that she's going through "The Change of Life." But Duvall, long-suffering good sport that he is, heroically stands by his wife throughout her pitiful breakdown.

Rent it some time. It ought to scare you. Did me.

There might be some woman like Duvall's wife somewhere out there, but in all the research and interviewing I've done, I've never met or heard of anyone even close. The problem is that the image stays with you. I can't remember the movie's name, but I sure remember her character.

Though Hollywood continues the myth of the crazy menopausal woman, they didn't create it. They usually build that kind of caricature around some picture we hold in our collective mind's eye. And for that picture to resonate with us, it must be built upon something that has in it at least a small kernel of truth.

Most menopausal women do go through something emotional. To that we can all agree. In this chapter we'll try to sort out first what some of these emotional changes might be, as well as look at what kinds of thoughts and feelings we can't attribute to menopause. Then we'll go on, in Chapters Six and Seven, to see if we can figure out where these changes come from and what to do about them.

What She's Likely to Feel

As with hot flashes and crawly skin, your wife may experience some of the following emotions, or maybe none of them. Remember that no two menopauses are alike. It's doubtful that she will feel all of what I'm about to describe, so relax; there's a good chance she'll experience only some of these effects.

Fatigue

Let's start with plain old tiredness. Even though fatigue is really a physical condition, it has a lot of emotional consequences. Anyone who's been robbed of sleep night after night by hot flashes is subject to feeling grumpy, on edge, and short-tempered.

Additionally, any of a woman's normal emotions may be intensified by lack of sleep. In fact, the intensification of preexisting feelings can be one of the biggest emotional effects of menopause.

Emotional Intensification

A common theme I've heard from many women is that, during menopause, nothing psychologically new comes up; the accustomed feelings are just felt more intensely.

Think of it: when you get wiped out, don't little things bug you? It'd be the same with anybody.

Women might have issues with themselves or with you that have lain dormant for years, just under the surface. Menopause, with all its ups and downs, can bring these issues into sharp focus. Perhaps your wife may have cut you some slack over the years for not helping around the house. But with the added stress and fatigue of menopause, she really needs your help. She may have been holding in her feelings as best she could for years, but some night when she's tired it might all come out at once. And you will sit there in front of the tube, mystified as to why she suddenly went mental.

It'll seem to you like you weren't doing anything any different from what you've always done. And you'll be right. The difference will be that, though she might always have been bothered, she managed before to keep her irritation under control for harmony's sake. The night she blows up will be the one when she just can't hold it in any longer. The eruption might seem irrational to you, but to her it will be completely logical—and justified.

The last thing your wife will want to hear is that what she's feeling isn't real, or isn't important. She could react as if she's been deeply insulted if you toss off a "You never thought like that before. You just feel that way because of menopause."

Menopause has not been seen to create fantasies. It's quite common, however, for it to make real feelings more intense.

While these menopausal feelings may not be especially comfortable at times, they can provide an opportunity for you and your wife to fine-tune important issues or even clean some old slates.

Overwhelmed

For years I've been teaching classes for Stephen Covey, based on his book *The Seven Habits of Highly Effective People.* The most common problem by far that both men and women talk about in these classes is that they feel overwhelmed—their lives are out of balance. It seems that, as a culture, we have too much to do, too many choices, too many things pulling us in too many different directions.

In the last few decades, women have been entering the workforce in ever-increasing numbers, adding full-time jobs to their already full plates. In return, we men have learned to cook, wash dishes, change diapers, and do the shopping. And that's great.

But in actuality we don't do much of this. Old roles, stereotypes, and expectations die hard.

As a result, our wives—and women in general—can feel much more stress than we men feel. And this is before you add in menopause. No wonder they might feel overwhelmed when hot flashes start.

Your wife might come home tired from work and see that she needs to run to the store before she can cook dinner. Normally she could take this in stride, but as she's standing there thinking about it, a hot flash starts sneaking up on her with some pre-flash anxiety. Suddenly she's worried but doesn't really know why. Then she has to sit down and ride out the flash, which causes her to feel even more drained. When the hot flash ends and she's regathering her energy, what looked just big before, i.e., shopping and cooking, might look monumental.

The advice here is pretty simple: If she's feeling overwhelmed, help her out. In many cases, the sharing of chores can be appreciated as much as empathy and understanding, if not more. It's an important way to show love, caring, and respect.

But be careful of the way you help. She won't want you to be condescending, but genuinely loving. She wants to know that you care, not that you think there's something wrong with her.

Anxiety

As I've mentioned, some women get to feeling anxious right before a hot flash starts. Until a woman has been through enough of them to connect the sudden angst with an impending flash, the feeling can be quite disorienting.

Imagine if something like this happened to you: You're doing whatever you're doing and all at once you're worried or afraid, sort of half paranoid, and you can't figure out why. You check everything out and there's nothing the matter. After you settle down, wham, it happens again. Imagine what you'd feel like if you got paranoid like this a few times an hour.

My wife put it this way: "I'd be going along just fine and then I'd get this kind of dread, like something was wrong, only I didn't know what it was. It came out of nowhere and would really throw me for a loop. After a while, though, I noticed that it came right before my hot flashes. Pretty soon I could recognize it and could relax, because all it meant was that I'd be flashing in a minute."

Susan learned to recognize the source of her feelings. If she hadn't, the unfounded anxiety could have been confusing, or even scary.

The greatest help you can offer here is awareness and support. This is a pretty tricky area. You need to recognize your partner's feelings for what they are: passing angst. But I wouldn't try to belittle her feelings at the moment she's feeling them by telling her they're not real—you know, like "Chill out. It's just menopause." Her feelings *are real.* It's just that they'll soon pass.

You can't make the angst go away any quicker, but you sure can make the situation worse. If she's anxious yet finds no reason for her fears, she'll probably make the connection between the feeling and a looming hot flash.

But if she's anxious and you feed her emotions by reacting, she'll probably make a connection between the feeling and *you.*

Mood Swings

About half of menopausal women report that they experience mood swings. These are emotions, feelings, or moods that come up and go away without any perceived external cause. In some women a mood swing might be as simple as pre-flash anxiety, but in others a mood might last for hours or even days before it shifts. Your wife's moods may even shift several times a day, leaving you wondering, "What is going on?"

• • •

For me, my wife's mood swings were the hardest part of her menopause. After her periods stopped, her moods would change unexpectedly. Before, I'd learned to time her PMS. Now I had no clue. One day she'd be nice, and the next, something else—maybe mad at me for some reason I couldn't begin to understand.

I was anything but an example of patience. I reacted. I floundered. I made it worse. It was not a pretty picture.

A fortunate coincidence helped me. At just about the same time my wife got her last period, my daughter got her first. My usually predictable daughter was suddenly different from day to day. I wasn't quite sure who I'd meet when I came home from work. Sometimes she was happy, bouncy, and outgoing; other times she'd be quiet and want to be alone.

Putting one and one together wasn't too difficult. I had a blinding flash of the obvious: both my daughter's and my wife's moods were being affected by their hormones.

I asked my daughter to read this chapter, and I really appreciate her advice here. She says, "I hate it when guys blame what I feel on my periods. It's not like I make up what I'm thinking. I just feel it a little more."

About menopause, she adds, "Since these moods are real, you better learn to deal with them."

One of the best ways I know of to deal with emotions is simply to be aware of them. If you want to be able to choose your response to whatever is happening around you or within you, awareness is crucial.

If all else fails, be patient. If your wife's moods are being affected by her fluctuating hormones, the intensity should pass with menopause. The issues that trigger the moods won't go away, but the intensity of the moodiness should.

Insecurity

Some menopausal women have reported that feelings of insecurity can unexpectedly arise in them. The insecurity can be temporary and pass quickly, kind of like the anxiety mentioned above, or it can stick around and deepen.

Some women are pretty strongly identified with how they look. If this is so, then—rightly or wrongly—the onset of menopause might trigger insecurity at the loss of their youthful image. And the insecurity could spread to worry about the loss of a job, or even a husband.

Some women might be made insecure by their emotional surges. They might be afraid that their anger or unpredictability will run off not only their husband, but maybe their whole family and their friends, too.

Some women might have complexes stemming from real situations in their childhood, like divorce or an absent parent. If a woman's hot flashes trigger insecurity, the insecurity might in turn trigger fears that spring from unconscious memories of abandonment or a not-so-fortunate youth.

Reassurance from you can help all of the above. But, if the fears run deep, your words might have a relatively small effect. To actually help your wife, you might have to demonstrate, repeatedly, that you love her.

Here, two-way communication is essential. I know that the

stereotype is that men don't like to talk about feelings, but you may need to be the one to open the door here. Encouraging your wife to talk about what's bothering her may be just what she needs in order to bring her issues into her awareness, so she can work through them. This may sound foreign or wrong or even dangerous to you, but don't worry about it. Just get ready to listen. I can almost guarantee you that it will be appreciated.

• • •

Even the people who believe that menopause does have emotional effects don't all agree about what causes these effects, or why some women experience them and some don't. Some say that changes in estrogen levels are the primary cause of mood swings; others aren't so sure.

In the next chapter, we'll take a look at the controversy about what causes the emotional changes. Is the source biological? That is, is it her fluctuating hormones or her general level of health? Or is it more attitudinal: her cultural conditioning, her self-image, or her feeling of being supported or being under a lot of stress? As you'll see, this is a complex issue, with no easy answers.

6 *T*he Causes of Mood Swings

Regarding the controversy about the origins of menopausal mood swings, authorities in the field mainly divide themselves into two camps. The first camp says that, because the fluctuating moods come from a woman's physiology, doctors can and should prescribe something with which to treat them. The second camp says that, because these moods derive from a woman's own thinking, from frail self-esteem, or from prevailing cultural attitudes, there's no need to try to treat them with medicine.

The Nature-or-Nurture Question

Here's what the positions of the two camps boil down to: menopausal mood swings come either from "nature," i.e., a woman's hormones and biology, or from "nurture," i.e., societal and attitudinal influences.

Some doctors and drug companies say that the emotions of menopause are caused by a lack of estrogen, and can be cured with pills and patches.

Their antagonists say that menopausal moods stem from belief systems, and that our culture is the culprit—that a woman's moods are caused by our patriarchal prejudices. For instance, if the society values a woman primarily as a mother, then her worth is diminished when she can no longer have babies. Consequently, when she reaches midlife her self-esteem may decline and she may exhibit a new moodiness.

Both sides of the argument have merit, but most people trying to make up their own minds about the question come down somewhere in between. In the simplest terms, it's likely that our culture *and* a woman's hormones combine to cause the many moods of menopause.

Distinguishing Moods From Depression

We are talking here about mood swings and emotional outbursts, not serious mental disorders. Again, while there are a lot of conditions that can be somehow tied to menopause, mental illness is not one of them.

Until the 1980s, women were sometimes diagnosed with a "disease" called "involutional melancholia." That was the clinical name for "the woman who goes nuts because of menopause." The medical establishment has now recognized the patronizing attitude toward women that gave rise to this diagnosis. They have corrected the error (and, to some extent, the attitude), and have stricken that label from the psychological texts.

Women don't go bonkers because of menopause. They may happen to get depressed or out of balance during menopause, but this won't happen because of it.

Let me repeat: *A lack of estrogen does not cause clinical depression, nor does an abundance of estrogen cure it.* Clinical depression results from a serious imbalance of neurochemicals. Conditions of this kind can often be effectively treated with drugs prescribed by a medical doctor. But the drugs prescribed for menopause are ineffective in treating this kind of brain disorder.

Mild depression is something most of us come up against from time to time. It is quite different from clinical depression.

Mild depression is a matter of moods, of feeling low, of having no energy or enthusiasm. Usually a psychologist can successfully treat this form of depression with any of a number of different kinds of therapies. Interestingly, some studies have shown that supplemental estrogen can help women with *mild* depression.

Take the Studies With a Grain of Salt

I need to say something about studies.

If, in reading this book, you happened to disagree with something that I say, you could probably support your argument by citing some study that has come up with contrary findings.

This points up a problem with menopause research at this stage of the game: there hasn't been enough of it. And, in a lot of cases, the research has been poorly done. Only recently have there been long-term, well-funded, double-blind scientific studies—you know, the kind where half the participants take a placebo, and none of the researchers knows which half is which.

I've heard at least three theories as to why there's been so little good research on menopause. One is that our baby boomer wives, who came of age during the sexual revolution and are more candid than previous generations, are the first wave of women to be openly interested. Another theory says that nobody was interested in menopause until the drug companies realized they could make a buck. And a third theory says that researchers only got busy when women, spurred by changing attitudes toward women's health and the medical profession, got worried about the long-term effects of treating something natural as if it were an illness.

Regardless, at this point there's little menopause data out there, and much of it is conflicting. But there will be much more in the near future. So, in an effort to be as accurate as possible, I will cite and refer to only the most conclusive and widely accepted data.

I suggest that you and your mate employ your minds, your feelings, your intuition, and some good old common sense in understanding the data and deciding how to respond to it.

Where Do Menopausal Moods Come From?

If estrogen can help with mild depression during menopause, then it makes some sense to think that a drop in estrogen might contribute to menopausal moods. But there are lots of other possible causes, too.

Our Youth-Centered Culture

There's no question that our culture places youth on an Olympian pedestal, and this is doubly so when it comes to women. If you don't believe me, the next time you go into the supermarket, check the covers on the women's magazines. Look at the pictures, then read the article titles on either side of that slim, sexy, computer-enhanced supermodel: "All about Beauty" . . . "In Search of the Perfect Plastic Surgeon" . . . "Who Is the American Ideal?" . . . "Uma Thurman, Today's Most Ravishing Woman." (I found all these titles on just one issue.)

Then thumb through the magazine and look at the ads. You'll see how women are being bombarded by unattainable images of youth and beauty: flawless faces, dangerously thin bodies, and unaffordably expensive clothes. The phenomenon is not limited to women's magazines; you'll see the same images in men's magazines and on signs and billboards, as well as in movies and TV shows.

Don't underestimate the subconscious power of these images. Their effects on us can be even more disturbing as we enter our mature years.

In many cultures, elders are venerated for their wisdom and cared for with pride by the younger generations. But in our society, elder care is often seen as an imposition. It's no wonder that many of us see aging as something to be feared and avoided.

So if menopause means to your wife that she's getting old, then it is sure to have an unconscious effect on how she feels about herself. This could be a major contributor to the feelings of insecurity we talked about before.

Even if you really work at it, you can't expect to easily undo all of society's influences. Cultural scripting dies hard. It's one thing to believe intellectually that aging is a good thing. It's another to have positive feelings about aging on a deep emotional level.

You can influence your wife's emotions here either way—positively or negatively. It might help her to hear you say how much you value the wisdom that comes with age, how you admire the character that shows in an older face. But she may not be convinced by words alone. You may have to show her through your example.

We all know that we need to take extra good care of ourselves as we get older. There's no question that a good diet and lots of exercise are key contributors to a long and active life. What *isn't* helpful is going overboard and obsessing about staying slim and buff.

You can be a real help to your spouse if you can *accept your own aging.* Exercise for fitness, not looks. Throw away your hair-coloring formula. Resist buying that 'Vette. Your actions will speak volumes, much more than anything you may say. You'll probably need to do some reassuring, but you'll also need to demonstrate how much you want to relax into your older years with your wife. You can do this by just being with her—spending time with her, listening to her, and sharing yourself with her—especially during menopause's more trying times.

The End of the "Mom" Role

As I mentioned near the start of this chapter, another cultural influence on a woman's feelings at menopause can be how much we value women in their roles as mothers, while minimizing their other contributions. In most parts of our culture, a woman is valued first and foremost as a mom.

Now, I have no quarrel with motherhood. Where would we be without it? But if a woman sees herself *only* as a mother—and sees nothing beyond that but the trash heap—what might that concept do to her self-esteem when she matures beyond the age of childbearing?

Since the female baby boomers have been out in the workforce for decades, they may not feel the loss of their childbearing years as strongly as their mothers' generation did. Not only have they borne children, but they have also pursued careers and developed other interests that will continue after their children are grown.

But don't think that the women of today are no longer affected by the ending of the childbearing years. Even women who have established their identities beyond the maternal role may still feel the impact of this transitional time. Remember that cultural messages about the importance of childbearing imprint themselves deeply. Be sensitive and supportive if you sense that your wife is feeling some loss.

The Empty Nest Syndrome

Going right along with the end of the "mom" role is what's popularly called "the empty nest syndrome." Not only is a woman losing her capacity to bear children, but the children she has raised may, during the same time period, be moving out of the house. If a woman is strongly identified with motherhood, this double whammy can upset her disposition in ways no self-help book can alleviate.

Since human biology requires that a woman eventually move beyond bearing children, menopause is a natural time of passage from one stage of life to another. But, as with all times of passage in our lives, we can be affected on pretty deep psychological and emotional levels, especially if we're reluctant to move on to the next stage. So, if a woman has felt herself fulfilled by motherhood, it's reasonable to expect that a newly empty nest could affect her moods.

But believe me, the empty nest syndrome is not confined to women. As I write this, our youngest child is preparing her college applications. She's not even applying to any school within a thousand miles of here. Knowing that I'm no longer going to be a dad in quite the same way puts me through changes, too.

Still, the empty nest syndrome has another side. The media make a lot of noise about it, like when Chelsea Clinton enrolled at Stanford, but surveys show that most of us are more than ready to have the kids launched. Women, especially, have mixed feelings during this transition, such as nostalgia and maternal attachment mixed with anticipation and new inklings of freedom.

If your wife seems profoundly affected by the flight of your children from the nest, you can help. For one thing, you can remind her (and yourself) that parenthood doesn't end just because the kids move out. As long as you have children, you will always be parents; you'll just be parents in a different way.

The Effect of Attitude

As I've mentioned, doctors no longer consider the moods of menopause to be "all in her head." But there is some interesting research that shows that a woman's mental attitude may affect her passage through the change. The research suggests that, just as those women who welcome motherhood have an easier pregnancy, women who look forward to menopause can have an easier time of it too. This line of reasoning conversely suggests that women who dread menopause, or who already suffer emotionally, may be subject to a harder passage.

One obvious conclusion of this research is that a woman's attitude can effect her menopausal moods. Accordingly, many of the popular books offer strategies for improving one's thinking and attitudes, and for generally taking charge of one's own menopause.

While all this sounds really good on the surface, this conclusion offers some challenges in at least two areas.

First of all, if you keep following this reasoning, you can argue that, if a good attitude makes the moods of menopause better, then a woman is *causing* her own bad moods with a bad attitude. Or, to put it a different way, we're right back at "It's all in her head." Thankfully, that old Freudian-type view has been discredited. And thanks to the fact that doctors now see both biology and psychology at work in the feminine midlife experience, women no longer risk facing mental institutions and shock treatments if they experience menopause as a difficult time.

Ironically, there's a small but vocal branch of the women's movement that has brought this argument back in a slightly different form. They would like us to believe that there's essentially no difference between women and men. They argue that a woman is not at the mercy of her hormones, or that if there are hormonal effects (some don't even admit this), a woman can overcome them with the strength of her mind and will. So, this reasoning concludes, with a strong enough application of her will, a woman needn't be affected by menopause. In other words, "It's all in her head."

The second challenge to the positive-attitude-as-a-fix-all argument is that sometimes, regardless of how strongly we believe, attitude adjustments simply don't work. Anyone who has tried to fix deep-seated psychological problems overnight or to change physical realities with affirmations and visualizations has some sense of this particular form of futility. These kinds of techniques can only work over time, and only when they are firmly built upon a bedrock of realistic—not wishful—thinking.

When a woman is led to believe that she can "fix" herself with affirmations, visualizations, and the use of disciplined willpower—and then these techniques don't work—she can take it personally, blame herself, and end up making things worse. Inappropriate guilt or shame can result from this perceived failure. The woman may conclude that there must be something wrong with *her*, rather than with the unrealistic technique she's using. Fortunately, most menopause authors are not prescribing a quick fix, because there isn't one.

Menopause is bigger than the mind and must run its course in its time. What a woman is going to experience in menopause is what she's going to experience. Having a positive attitude won't "cure" menopause. But developing an awareness of her moods and attitudes can mean that a woman may be able to have more choices about how she responds to what happens to her.

Brain Chemistry

Recently, scientists have begun to show some interesting connections between the chemicals in our brains and how we feel. The research has been conducted only since the 1970s, but by now most of us have heard about endorphins, the body's own morphine-like substances that make us feel good. The research has been broadened to look for connections between female hormones and menopausal moods, and the connections seem to be there.

We are still in the early stages of neurochemical science, but one connection that has already been shown is between estrogen and endorphins. It's a complex relationship, but it seems that added estrogen can stimulate the hypothalamus gland to release endorphins, with the result that a woman feels better. Recent research has begun to show many more connections between neurochemicals and human moods, such as the links between dopamine and the feeling of joy; between serotonin and sadness; between acetycholine and angst. My guess is that, in the not-too-distant future, researchers will be able to show exactly how the ups and downs of hormones such as estrogen and progesterone affect the neurochemicals that, in turn, affect moods.

Recent research has also suggested that low estrogen levels might cause the synapses between cells in the brain to function at a diminished capacity. Synapses are the spaces between neurons, or nerve cells, that allow messages to be transferred from one cell to another. It is believed that estrogen might assist this message transfer. Lower levels of estrogen in the brain might, therefore, contribute to the loss of reasoning power and short-term memory that some women experience during menopause.

My wife has always had a sharp mind; losing her teacup ("Check the microwave, Susan") or being unable to balance the checkbook can lead to unaccustomed frustration for her. I imagine that if a woman were not aware, as Susan is, that her hormonal state can cause these mental lapses, she might feel worried and insecure about her own mental functioning.

Early findings have shown that heightened estrogen levels can repair the synapses and improve short-term memory. Conversely, though, without estrogen the synapses will eventually repair themselves.

A few studies have shown promise that estrogen supplements may help fend off Alzheimer's Disease in postmenopausal women. It is not known whether giving estrogen to men would have the same effect. (Remember that an increase of estrogen seemed to reduce the incidence of heart disease in women, but increased it in men.) Again, the research in this area is only in its beginning stages.

Some women feel comforted when they learn about the connection between hormones and moods—that is, when they learn that their changing hormones can intensify their emotional changes. They find assurance in being aware of the effects their body is having on their feelings. Other women are grateful to know that they can choose to take HRT for relief if they need to.

Although it is still too early to draw any sweeping conclusions about women's feelings, it seems reasonable to suppose that both our ingrained cultural attitudes and a woman's physiology contribute to menopause's emotional ups and downs. But one important question remains: If menopause causes intense feelings, is that really a problem?

What's Wrong With Feelings, Anyway?

One of the subtle but pervasive legacies of our rational, left-brained culture is the idea that there is something wrong—even dangerous—about feelings and emotions.

Could there be a beneficial reason for feelings? Could they possibly have evolved to serve some good purpose?

Many women with whom I've talked feel glad for menopause's intensified season of emotions. They insist that the buried psychological material uncovered by this passage has been valuable to their growth.

These women say that, without the intensification of feelings brought on by menopause, they might never have had the chance to deal with important, deep-seated issues. While the resulting growth process wasn't easy or fun, when they got to the other side of it these women were grateful for what they had learned.

If your wife is one who, like so many women of our generation, is open to personal growth, she may see menopause as more of an opportunity than a problem. She may actually feel fortunate that, through the unusual force of her feelings, her psyche is bringing long-hidden issues to the surface.

What About Your Feelings?

You, however, may see menopausal moodiness differently. If you're like I was, you might want to fix it, and fast. The challenge here is to realize that, since there's really nothing broken, there's nothing to fix. There is nothing the matter with your wife; she's just going through menopause.

So why not try backing off and letting her transition run its course? Why not try being understanding and supportive?

"Well," you might answer, "because I have feelings too. Sometimes she really ticks me off. Is this all just about letting her do her thing? What about me?" These are good questions, ones that I asked myself a lot.

"No," I would answer, "it's not all just about her. Before you blow up, you need to express yourself too."

No relationship can be one-sided, if it is to have any chance of working. What's important, though, is how you express yourself, such as trying to say what you need to say considerately. We'll talk more about that in Chapter Twelve.

• • •

We've looked at quite a few factors that influence a woman's menopause, but one area we haven't yet covered is how the medical "industry" has tried to claim this life passage as its own domain. The medicalization of menopause is such a powerful and controversial issue that I have devoted the entire next chapter to the subject.

7
*T*he Medicalization of Menopause

Perhaps the most demeaning aspect of our cultural programming about aging is the prevailing "medicalization" of menopause. We have subtly but surely come to believe that menopause, something every woman goes through, requires a doctor's care.

There is no denying that menopause can cause problems that may need attention. But allow me to repeat that *menopause is not unnatural, nor is it a disease.*

I have tried to keep the words "symptom" and "cure" entirely out of our discussions (except in quotes or italics). Only illnesses have symptoms. Only something medically wrong needs a cure. Menopause, by contrast, is normal—maybe not entirely pleasant, but normal, natural, and universal.

Your wife may be reading any of a number of books that tackle this subject with a fury. You should know, at least generally, what's being said in those books. I must acknowledge that what follows is tinged by my personal feelings, because I believe that we, as a society, are way off base when we stigmatize all middle-aged women as having an illness that needs treatment.

Who Is to Blame?

Many different people and institutions could be blamed for influencing us, as a culture, to look upon menopause as a disease. In truth, all of the following may share in the culpability. We'll look at these possible culprits one by one.

Is It Robert Wilson?

For the last hundred years or so, Western physicians have tried their best to "treat" menopause. Mostly it's been out of the goodness of their hearts. After all, doctors are by and large a good lot; they work hard to relieve human suffering. The problem is in the way they see this feminine transition. It's their paradigm of menopause that we need to question.

Ever since Robert Wilson's 1963 book, *Feminine Forever*, we as a populace have carried the bias that menopause is a "deficiency disease," like diabetes, that requires treatment. Wilson was the first to peg menopause as a disease that stemmed from a physiological deficiency. His immensely popular and widely quoted book set the tone for many that followed it, even though he and the ideas set down in *Feminine Forever* have since been discredited.

For decades after Wilson published his book, doctors writing in journals and in subsequent books followed his lead, describing menopausal women as "pitiful creatures" whose "dismal and catastrophic changes" include "ovarian failure" and "diseased areas" like "atrophied genitalia," "senile vaginitis," and "dead gonads." (I kid you not—these are direct quotes.)

Here's more: In menopause, a woman's "loss of feminine functions" causes a "vapid cow-like feeling." She becomes "hump-backed" and her vagina becomes "a dry, rigid tube." She gets "flabby, wrinkled" breasts with skin that "coarsens and is covered with scales."

How about this one? At menopause she becomes "a shriveled shell of a woman, used up, sucked dry, desexed, and, by comparison with her treasured remembrances of bygone days of glory and romance, fit only for the bone heap."

These are the actual statements of so-called experts. Do you understand why I believe that this kind of thinking degrades women?

If you want to find further quotes like this, see Mary Lou Logothetis's essay, on pages 40–45, in *Women of the 14th Moon: Writings on Menopause*, edited by Dena Taylor and Amber Sumrall. I loved this book, which is an excellent collection of stories, poetry, and essays about menopause.

It turns out that Robert Wilson's research foundation was funded by the very same pharmaceutical companies that made and sold the drugs Wilson said were needed at menopause. As soon as the public got wind of this connection, the evident conflict of interest caused a loss of confidence in both Wilson and his research. No longer was he lauded and quoted—yet considerable damage had already been done.

Wilson had long been a tireless and charismatic crusader for his cause (which, in his defense, he probably believed would do women some good). His influence far outlasted his fifteen minutes of fame. As a result, he not only set the prevailing menopause paradigm; he was also largely responsible for creating a whole new sector of commerce, "the menopause industry."

Is It Western Medicine?

Many people would like to blame the Western medical tradition for our outdated ideas about menopause. And it's true that Western doctors tend to think like mechanics. If there's a problem, find the cause and fix it. Symptoms are what they look for. Trace a symptom back to its cause, find something that's gone wrong, dig into your tool kit, and voilà. When you find the right tool, you've got a cure.

Like any other kind of technician, a Western doctor will use what's in his or her kit. If drugs are all that's in there, then that's what a Western doctor will use. They believe in them. That's how they've been trained.

But it's how they perceive menopause that's the problem. Robert Wilson suggested that doctors see menopause as a deficiency disease caused by ovarian failure. And he put estrogen in their tool kits.

A better way to see this transition might be to view it as a fulfillment that is to be followed by a new beginning. Why not see menopause as the culmination of one stage of a woman's biological life, a stage during which her ovaries have fulfilled one of their functions?

Since doctors have been conditioned to see ovarian failure rather than fulfillment, they see menopause as something that's broken.

Should We Blame the Drug Companies?

Without question, the pharmaceutical industry is partly responsible for the medicalization of menopause. But the drug companies aren't all peopled by profiteers. Some people ascribe evil intentions to these multinational megacorporations, but I've had the privilege of working directly with some drug researchers, and I've come to the conclusion that there's hardly a more inspired group of people anywhere. They really believe that their work will help relieve human suffering.

Then again, there's no doubt that the companies and their executives are responsible to their shareholders for a return on their investments. There's a profit motive somewhere in every company, so we need to be aware and informed.

Profit is not evil; it's a necessary end for anybody in business. We might as well accept profit's existence and influence. But, in the absence of moral restraint, the drive to increase profit can be a powerful force that moves individuals and organizations to use questionable means to achieve their ends.

This is a hot issue among menopause writers. You should be

aware that quite a few menopause books—especially those that question the wisdom of HRT—are raising these kinds of concerns. Some authors are downright accusatory, blaming the drug companies for a host of problems ranging from quickly tested drugs that later cause cancer to mass media marketing that touts youthful images to entice consumers to buy patches and pills.

• • •

Just for your information, let me give you a thumbnail sketch of how we get a lot of our new drugs these days. Researchers are always looking for chemical compounds that are active in fighting disease. In their search, they have even gone into the rain forests to find traditional healers who will show them what has worked for centuries.

When the researchers find an active ingredient, they try to isolate it in order to duplicate it, altering it just slightly for patent purposes. Then they try out the new compound in a test tube or petri dish to make sure it works, then on animals, watching for side effects. If the drug is safe enough, they apply to the FDA, then do their trials on humans, again watching out for side effects.

If, after the testing, it looks as if the benefits will outweigh the risks, the FDA approves the drug and the pharmaceutical company markets it to you and me, in the hope of making our lives better.

The whole process is expensive. In order to recoup their research costs and make a profit, the companies need to protect their new drugs with patents. You can't patent nature—that's why the chemicals are always made to differ a little from the way they were when originally found.

For the most part, the system works and benefits humankind. Arguably, some of the greatest improvements in the quality of human life in the 20th century have come from advances in medicine. But there can be problems. Some side effects of the drugs don't show up for quite a while—for decades or even generations. And there's also greed, which, sad to say, researchers and their companies occasionally succumb to, putting the bottom line ahead of caution.

As I said before, undoubtedly the fault for *some* of the medicalization of menopause lies with the pharmaceutical companies. A good question to ask might be this: How much is our cultural attitude toward menopause being influenced by the drug companies' annual reports to stockholders?

Doctors, Doctors, Doctors

Since nothing can be done in the short term about the medicalization of menopause, your wife will probably consult a physician at some point—if not to ask about some of the effects she's feeling, at least at the time of her annual checkup and pap test. Her choice of a doctor is an important decision, for the health care professional she chooses will be one of the most influential people your spouse deals with during her menopause.

Ordinarily, a woman won't go see a doctor about a missed period or two. She'll wait until something is really bothering her—maybe a lot of bleeding, some serious hot flashes, or several missed periods in a row. Many women, when they finally do suspect menopause, will go to their doctor just to find out what's happening.

In this age of HMOs, a typical annual visit may be with a "primary care physician." These doctors are the new incarnation of the "family doctor"—generalists with knowledge about a broad range of medicine. Because the topic of menopause has been appearing in their literature quite a bit lately, primary care physicians are likely to know some of the latest news.

Usually these doctors will have a discussion with a new menopause patient to assess the severity of her "symptoms," and they may order some blood or urine tests to measure her estrogen levels. If the tests determine that a woman is menopausal, the primary care physician may continue to treat her or may choose to refer her to a gynecologist (an OB-GYN).

This brings up a potential problem: the inadequacy of some testing procedures. As I said before, I was blissfully misled into denial when my wife's blood test results indicated she was not in menopause. The doctor said that her estrogen levels were normal. Fortunately, medical science has progressed since then.

It turns out that a single blood test can miss quite a lot of information. Not only do hormone levels fluctuate throughout a monthly cycle; they can also vary widely in the course of a single day. Many doctors now realize that they should be taking more than one sample. Because it's inconvenient to take blood all day long, urine and saliva have become the preferred sampling sources. If your wife's doctor isn't aware of this, you could be misled just as I was.

Another challenge with a single test, even if it is a full day's sampling, is that there is no baseline measurement to compare it to. Not only do women's hormones go through various cycles; it's also very tricky to try to compare one woman to a norm. Optimally, before any prescriptions are issued (or at least before they're reissued), a whole series of daylong tests will have been taken in order to determine the normal hormone levels. The best thing of all would be to have taken tests prior to menopause, but this is usually not practical.

Because this whole area is so iffy, the best doctors don't rely solely on tests. They also use some old-fashioned diagnostic tools: questions and answers. Your wife's visit to her doctor should include a fairly in-depth interview.

There is opportunity for a husband to be of some help in this process (although by the time you've picked up this book, your wife has probably long since gone this far down the doctor path).

I encourage you to discuss with your mate the advice she may be receiving from her doctors. She could be faced with tough and far-reaching decisions, such as whether to take hormones or undergo a hysterectomy.

Again, of course, you should be primarily in the listening mode. You need to work hard here to understand your wife's concerns and fears. I'd be very cautious about making pronouncements about what you think she should do, but you could offer something like, "Is that your only choice?" or "What about asking another doctor?"

It's critical to examine all the options around such decisions as whether to have a hysterectomy or to start hormone replacement therapy.

Sources of Second Opinions

Before making any major decision, obtaining a second opinion is advisable. If your spouse wants help, you can do some of the legwork to find out where she can get alternative professional guidance.

Clinics That Specialize in Women's Health

Doctors who specialize in women's health have traditionally been males. Obstetricians and gynecologists, or OB-GYNs, are now more and more often female, and to a lot of menopausal women this is good news. While not necessarily more compassionate, female OB-GYNs certainly have a better opportunity for shared experience.

It is not uncommon for these doctors to band together into clinics that specialize in all areas of women's health. Chances are that there is a women's health clinic near you that would be covered in some way under your wife's insurance plan. All you have to do to be of help here is look in your local Yellow Pages. Here are some other phone numbers that might be useful for referrals:

The North American Menopause Society, (216) 844-3334

The National Women's Health Network, (202) 628-7814

The Holistic Doctors of ACAM

A small but growing number of M.D.s and osteopaths are approaching medicine holistically. That is, they consider the whole person as they make their diagnoses and write their prescriptions. Most of us have heard of the mind-body connection, which refers to the idea that the mind affects whether we get sick or how fast we heal. That's the kind of thing these holistic physicians look at.

These practitioners take lots of time with their patients, listening to more than just physical symptoms. They tend to know more than the strictly allopathic physicians about things like herbs, acupuncture, and natural hormones.

While there are not yet a great many of them, these doctors have a respected professional organization, the American College for Advancement in Medicine (ACAM). For a referral, call (800) 532-3688.

Osteopaths

Osteopathic physicians, or D.O.s, go through graduate and residency training that is identical to what M.D.s go through—with the addition of hundreds more hours of training in the structure of the body and how it effects healing and wellness. You and your wife might find an osteopath who, like an M.D., can serve as her primary care physician or OB-GYN. Osteopaths can and do prescribe drugs and perform surgery, but this is not their preferred course of action. They usually conduct their practice of medicine from a different philosophy, one that places more emphasis on looking at the whole person and treating the body's structural systems.

If your wife sought treatment from an osteopath, she could expect him or her to endeavor to bring her various systems into balance by working with the musculoskeletal system as a foundation. A D.O. would likely do a structural examination of her body and posture, take X rays, do bone-density tests, and conduct extensive interviews with your wife about her history, diet, lifestyle, exercise, and general conditioning before prescribing any course of menopausal treatment.

Osteopathic therapy may include hormone replacements, but may also include nutrition, exercise, and natural remedies. Especially if your wife is at high risk for osteoporosis (if she is Asian or Caucasian, small-boned, and has a family history of osteoporosis), an osteopath may be an excellent choice. These doctors can be found in the Yellow Pages under "Physicians"; look for "D.O." after the doctor's name instead of "M.D." Or you can call the American Osteopathic Association at (312) 202-8000 for a referral.

Naturopaths and Chiropractors

If a woman is going to get a second or third opinion about something like HRT, it's often best to find a source that is as unrelated to the source of the first opinion as possible. If your wife got her original information from her regular doctor, there are some very different sources that she can access.

Although many insurance companies and the American Medical Association might have us think otherwise, naturopaths and chiropractors are well-trained medical professionals who achieve excellent results in their areas of expertise. Many caring and qualified individuals in each of these professions are knowledgeable about menopause and can help a woman address its challenges.

Naturopaths. Naturopaths, or N.D.s, are also board-certified physicians with four years of medical school and further residencies. The emphasis in naturopathic study and training is not so much on how drugs heal the body as how the body heals itself. N.D.s work holistically with all of the body's systems to prevent disease and optimize wellness. Naturopaths might also look for the mind-body connection, because they acknowledge the potential of the mind and spirit to create both disease and wellness.

A naturopathic physician being consulted by a menopausal woman would schedule an extensive first appointment to assess her general health and health history, including her current diet and exercise program and her mental and emotional state. The diagnosis period would include interviews and tests to determine her risk for osteoporosis, cardiovascular disease, and cancer.

Although N.D.s can prescribe drugs, most tend to use alternatives to the standard allopathic drugs and treatments available through our customary medical system. A naturopath's last two years of medical school focus on herbal remedies, nutrition, and physical medicine such as therapeutic massage.

Rather than handing out mass-produced pamphlets or prescribing standardized formulas, naturopaths take care to customize their treatments to the patient, believing that everyone is an individual. A naturopathic "prescription" would most likely include specific recommendations for diet, exercise, vitamins, minerals, homeopathic remedies, and perhaps natural hormone supplementation.

In most states, naturopaths can prescribe all types of drugs to their patients, but in some states N.D.s are allowed to offer only nonprescription drugs. If an N.D. practicing in one of the restrictive states determines that a woman needs hormone replacement therapy, he or she will at least be able to help her find natural hormones. To locate a naturopath in your area, call the American Association of Naturopathic Physicians at (206) 298-0126.

Chiropractors. Most of us are familiar with chiropractors and the effectiveness of their treatments to help realign a damaged or misaligned spine. Even many regular M.D.s acknowledge that chiropractic medicine offers benefits. Like other physicians, chiropractic doctors, or D.C.s, also go through extensive graduate and postgraduate training and testing before they are officially certified and licensed.

Many chiropractors have chosen to follow the path of holistic medicine and have gained additional knowledge and experience in massage, nutrition, the mind-body connection, and the analysis of blood for deficiencies. Like a naturopath, a chiropractor is likely to conduct a lengthy initial interview, to order blood tests, and to prescribe a customized alternative menopausal treatment. The treatment might include herbs, vitamins, natural hormones, and various types of adjustments and body work. Chiropractors have been so well-established professionally for so long that they have their own heading in the Yellow Pages. If you need a referral, contact the American Chiropractic Association at (703) 276-8800.

Hysterectomies

In all my research for this book, I was most shocked by the statistic that *half of the women over fifty in the United States have had a hysterectomy*—a surgery that removes the uterus and often the ovaries as well.

Their History and Current Status

The history of hysterectomies reflects the unfortunate view that Western medicine has had of women. Way back in Ancient Greece, Hippocrates, our "father of medicine," summed up what would become a dominant bias for a couple of millennia.

"What is woman?" Hippocrates was asked.

"Disease," was his answer.

By the mid 1800s, women's ovaries and uterus were targeted as the origin of their "disease," and were blamed not only for menstrual problems but also for sinfulness, suicide, obesity, sexuality, tuberculosis, masturbation, promiscuity, unwelcome emotions, the reading of romantic novels, and, of course, hysteria.

The hysterectomy epidemic really got going in the United States in the second half of the 20th century, as part of the medicalization of menopause. In his 1969 book *Hysterectomy: Past, Present, and Future*, Robert Wright wrote, "After the last planned pregnancy the uterus becomes a useless . . . organ and therefore should be removed." Like those of his contemporary, Robert Wilson, Wright's views are much less popular today, but the effect of his kind of thinking is still profoundly felt.

It is strange that the hysterectomy craze hasn't caught on in the rest of the world, even in other industrialized countries. For every five hysterectomies in the U.S., there are two in England and one in Sweden. Only about 25 percent of the hysterectomies in the United States are nonelective, i.e., necessary. I'm trying to be charitable here. Dr. Stanley West, in his book *The Hysterectomy Hoax*, makes a convincing argument that only 10 percent are medically necessary.

Routine hysterectomies performed in the belief that a uterus is no longer needed and is potentially troublesome are preventative surgeries that remove healthy organs. We are second-guessing nature here, which is always an iffy idea. Taking out the ovaries with the uterus as a precaution against cancer used to be almost standard procedure. This would be equivalent to having a doctor remove your testicles—that is, castrate you—to avoid whatever slim chance you might have of getting cancer later in your life. Ouch!

The hysterectomies we've been performing in the U.S. have been "castrating" women on a huge scale—roughly one-third of all American women in the last three to four decades. But now we're learning that a woman's ovaries remain important to her system long after menopause—virtually all of her life.

Whoops.

Fortunately, in the 1980s doctors began to wake up. But not all the way. At the end of that decade, more than 40 percent of all hysterectomies still included removal of the ovaries. Today, your wife is less likely to be confronted with the possibility of needlessly losing her perfectly good ovaries. Still, she has a 50 percent chance of being told that she should have her uterus removed.

Hysterectomies carry all the risks of any major surgery performed under general anesthesia, and more. Up to 80 percent of women who have hysterectomies are affected after the surgery by postoperative trauma. About 70 percent experience hot flashes, even if they keep their ovaries. Bladder problems and sexual discomfort are common, although usually temporary. A potentially long-term problem occurs when, in the absence of the uterus, other organs settle into the newly vacant abdominal space, causing an out-of-place bladder or bowel.

Also troubling following hysterectomies are reports of prolonged instances of anxiety, depression, melancholia, sexual dysfunction, ovarian failure, and loss of libido. Perhaps most troubling is the increase in heart disease that ensues. It seems that the uterus, as well as the ovaries, helps keep a healthy heart. Because these organs continue to produce hormones even after menopause, removing them can have profound effects on a woman's body. A hysterectomy is most definitely not "just a simple operation."

To present a balanced picture, I should say that necessary hysterectomies are truly beneficial. They help with urinary problems, vaginal bleeding, and uterine growths of many kinds. Most of all, they can stop cancer. If your wife comes home talking about getting one, you'd better listen up. Second and third opinions would be more than advisable.

If you want more information, I recommend Chapter Nine of *Menopause: A Guide for Women and Those Who Love Them* by Cutler and Garcia. The book, including the hysterectomy chapter, is pretty well balanced. If you want the negative view, read *The Hysterectomy Hoax* by Stanley West, M.D. I'm not aware of any books that champion hysterectomies, though there may be some out there.

• • •

There is one last area where Western medicine plays a major role in menopause: hormone supplementation. In the next chapter, we'll look at the toughest decision your wife is likely to face during her menopause: whether or not to take HRT.

8 *T*he Great Hormone Controversy

T he most contentious question today concerning menopause is the debate over whether a woman should or
should not take hormones. This is likely to be a difficult
decision for your wife, particularly because she will hear so
many different stories and opinions. She very well may want to
talk it over with you.

To Take or Not to Take

The whole question of the use of hormone replacement therapy has provoked a controversy that's not likely to be resolved
any time soon. Studies that might shed some light on the pros
and cons of HRT won't be completed until well into the next
century. In the meantime, individuals whose opinions have
placed them at either extreme of the controversy are taking
some pretty entrenched and uncompromising positions.

It's hard for anyone to remain neutral, because our positions
tend to come from deeply held values and convictions. Your
family history, your experience with the medical community,
and your fears and philosophies about life can influence how
you feel about HRT as much as or more than all the studies of
medical science.

Both the issue and your wife's choices are complex and full of gray areas. There are both drawbacks and benefits to the use of HRT; there are short-term and long-term options; there are alternatives such as diet, herbs, and acupuncture; and now there are natural hormone replacements. Making a decision can involve much information gathering, discussion, and reflection.

Caution and Healthy Skepticism

Something as complicated as the hormonal balance in a woman's bloodstream needs to be seen in the context of a very large picture—within the scope of evolution, for starters. There may be perfectly good biological reasons why menopause has developed during the course of human evolution, so medical tinkering should be done with care.

Lewis Thomas, renowned physician and beloved author, wrote a wonderful essay entitled "Autonomy" in his prize-winning book *The Lives of a Cell*. In the essay, Thomas expressed the awe with which he regards the complexity of the human body, saying how glad he is that he doesn't have to be responsible for taking over the running of even something as simple as his liver: "Nothing would save me and my liver if I were in charge. For I am, to face the facts squarely, considerably less intelligent than my liver. I am moreover constitutionally unable to make hepatic decisions. . . . I would not be able to think of the first thing to do. . . . I have the same feeling about the rest of my working parts. They are all better off without my intervention. . . . I'd rather leave all of my automatic functions with as much autonomy as they please, and hope for the best."

We should be so humble. Isn't it a bit presumptuous of us to think that we have the wisdom to try to direct the functioning of our delicate internal systems?

It is always wise to be cautious about introducing any powerful substance, whether prescribed or sold over the counter, into one's body. Doctors can too easily prescribe a patch or a pill for menopause, in the belief that it will "cure" a woman's "symptoms." Indeed, hormone replacements have some well-documented benefits, but we should approach any drug with healthy skepticism.

There are possible dangers as well, such as side effects. If we add a hormone into a system that is far more complex than our liver, we might not know for quite a while that we've caused an unintended chain of events. I personally have had such an experience with questionable "wonder drug wisdom."

While pregnant, my mother was given DES, a hormone that was supposed to "cure" her morning sickness. A generation later, researchers discovered that the daughters of the women who took DES during pregnancy are at increased risk for uterine and cervical cancer. More recently, almost two generations later, researchers have realized that DES sons are at risk too, of prostate cancer. I have no doubt that, at the time, doctors believed they were helping. They simply didn't know the long-term effects of their prescriptions.

Sometimes it's wiser to leave the systems to themselves and, as Thomas said, "hope for the best." At the very least we need to be cautious and skeptical, and to take care not to rush to try every new wonder drug or even every highly touted herbal remedy.

My own experience is a testament to caution. This doesn't mean that I feel that women should not take hormones at menopause, just that they should gather a lot of information and explore all their options.

A Brief History of HRT

The connection between estrogen and the ovaries was established soon after hormone research began in the 1930s. Back then, estrogen replacement was prescribed only for women who had undergone hysterectomies that included the ovaries.

When a woman was surgically thrown into premature menopause this way, her body would react immediately. The drop in estrogen created the usual effects: hot flashes, irritability, etc. The taking of estrogen replacements countered these effects quite dramatically.

In the 1960s, Robert Wilson made a seemingly logical connection: if estrogen helped women undergoing surgically induced menopause, it would probably help women going through natural menopause, as well. So he found some menopausal women who were willing to be test subjects, gave them estrogen supplements, saw similar good results, and wrote his book.

Initially, Wilson built his case around the idea of keeping a woman *Feminine Forever* (that, you'll recall, was the title of his book). He and his contemporaries maintained that supplemental estrogen could restore a woman's "intrinsic social value [that] plummets at menopause."

Thankfully, few people are writing like that any more—both women and men find it too repulsive. But because of the wide acceptance of Wilson's book, a headlong rush to prescribe estrogen for menopause was on. Wilson and the pharmaceutical companies were so successful that, within a few years, estrogen was one of the top five drugs prescribed in the United States.

The first danger sign came in the 1970s when a link between ERT (or estrogen replacement therapy, as it was then called) and uterine cancer was established.

Doctors, not wanting to do anything that could cause cancer, immediately stopped prescribing estrogen. A few years later, drug company researchers discovered that the cancer risk was mediated by the addition of progesterone, another female hormone, to estrogen. They call this "opposing" the estrogen, or "estrogen opposition." The companies created progestin, a synthetic progesterone, and changed the regimen's name to "*hormone* replacement therapy." The rush was on again, because by this time researchers had begun to establish other benefits of estrogen.

Today, the top-selling drug in the United States is Premarin, an estrogen that's produced from a mare's urine. During the cancer scare years, HRT advertising disappeared. Today

Premarin, usually combined with the progestin Provera, is back. Occasionally you will catch ads for HRT on a TV program that attracts middle-aged audiences.

The Two Sides

The two basic HRT positions are these:

- One side says that a woman should replace the hormones she loses during menopause to relieve her worst symptoms, such as hot flashes and vaginal dryness, and to decrease her chances of a heart attack and osteoporosis.

- The other side says that she shouldn't take hormones because of an increased risk of breast, uterine, and ovarian cancer and a lack of knowledge about long-term effects, and also because menopause is natural and we shouldn't monkey around with nature.

HRT's Benefits

Hormone replacement therapy wouldn't be popular if it didn't do any good. It can help menopausal women counteract many physical challenges, from hot flashes to heart attacks. The women who are helped by HRT are often vocal champions of it, and with good reason.

It Delays Osteoporosis

Taking estrogen slows bone loss. Pure and simple. It works.

Over the years, research has continued to document in ever more detail the ability of estrogen to prevent osteoporosis. It truly does keep the bones from thinning, lessening the chances of broken hips and cracked vertebrae in elderly women. Again, the only problem is the temporary nature of the benefit. Bone loss is slowed for only as long as a woman keeps taking HRT.

It Seems to Hold Off Heart Disease

Ever since researchers noticed that heart attacks increase in women after menopause, they've been trying to figure out why. Heart disease is complicated, having to do with diet, blood pressure, good and bad cholesterol, and so forth.

That's where HRT comes in. Since estrogen seems to be able to lower the level of so-called bad cholesterol and raise the amount of the good kind, logic would tell us that taking estrogen replacements would lead to fewer heart attacks.

• • •

Just the benefits in these two areas alone have convinced many doctors that HRT is the correct choice for menopausal women. These doctors are prescribing hormones for healthy women to keep them that way. They see long-term benefits and advocate long-term use of the drugs.

Heart disease is the major killer of postmenopausal women, and a broken hip caused by osteoporosis can put a woman in a wheelchair or even lead to death. But these two areas of health are not the only ones in which HRT can help.

It Can Mean No More Hot Flashes

As I mentioned before, some benefits of HRT are more obvious and immediate: supplemental estrogen has been found to stop hot flashes, night sweats, heart palpitations, and crawly skin.

This benefit alone is enough for those women who've decided in favor of HRT just because they want to make their passage through menopause more bearable. The 10 to 15 percent of women who are wiped out physically by hot flashes and night sweats can in this way get some major relief.

"I got my life back," one woman told me.

It Can Help a Woman Keep Her Career Going Strong

Other women choose HRT to make work more manageable. Many of our wives and their contemporaries are just hitting their stride in their careers when the hot flashes start.

A heavy-duty hot flash can be embarrassing, if not downright incapacitating. Sweaty, sleepless nights can make a woman tired and inefficient at work. Pre-hot flash anxiety can be distracting enough to ruin a woman's concentration. If severe and in combination, these menopausal effects can lower a woman's productivity. As a precaution, many women choose to take hormones rather than take the chance of having their careers suffer.

Also, it's sad to say but there's still enough prejudice and condescension from the "old-boy network" to cause a woman to head to her doctor for a prescription. The lingering attitudes may arise from a simple lack of understanding about hot flashes and fatigue. If a woman's menopause is misunderstood, she may be subjected to poor performance reviews and even to jokes, when what she needs is understanding and support.

Interestingly, though, awareness of menopause in the workplace environment is gradually growing. Some women are reporting that they are beginning to receive a bit of compassion. Perhaps this portends a shift in attitude.

It Can Give More Energy and Better Moods

While there is no conclusive evidence of this, some studies have shown that supplemental estrogen can lift a woman's moods and give her more energy. Again, estrogen doesn't work on serious depression, but it seems to help with the day-to-day ups and downs.

I thought the "more energy" part of HRT's benefits had to do with getting more sleep because of fewer night sweats, but there's some interesting anecdotal evidence that comes from women who have become women through sex-change operations and estrogen supplements. They get emotionally hooked on what they call their "happy pills."

Here's a quote from the hermaphroditic Lady Chablis in John Berendt's book *Midnight in the Garden of Good and Evil*. She's just been given a shot of estrogen, and she says, "Y-e-e-e-s, child, Miss Myra's shots are startin' to do their thing. I'm feelin' that boost of energy. . . . "

It Allows for Better Sex

HRT can restore the walls of a woman's vagina to their premenopausal plumpness and lubrication. A locally applied estrogen cream can also produce this effect. Some women who don't want to take HRT feel it's worth using the cream to receive this benefit alone.

This is where that advice in Chapter Four about estrogen creams comes in again. Be careful. The creams are not made to be used as lubricants. Your wife shouldn't be applying them right before sex. Unless, of course, you want to absorb the estrogen into your body and turn out like the Lady Chablis.

So Why Wouldn't a Woman Take HRT?

Because of all its known benefits, many doctors have a hard time understanding why only about one-fourth of American women take HRT. The lower risk of heart disease alone should be enough, they figure, to cause women to request prescriptions. But there are many reasons why women don't take HRT.

It May Be That She's Unaware or Unaffected

Despite the media blitz, about 60 percent of women are simply unaware of HRT as an option. The women who do take hormones tend to be better educated and from the middle class. Often the news hasn't yet reached women who don't have a college education or easy access to medical care.

Also, many women—up to one-half of them—are not sufficiently affected to ever visit their doctors about menopause. They don't take hormones because menopause is not a big issue in their lives.

But many other women, who are both aware of HRT and affected by menopause, cite numerous other reasons for choosing not to take hormones.

It May Be the Threat of Cancer

Probably the most pervasive reason that women give for not taking estrogen is the lingering fear of cancer, and not just uterine cancer. During approximately the same years that ERT and HRT have been in vogue, the incidence of breast cancer in women has risen from one in fourteen to one in nine. A Swedish study conducted in the 1980s found a link between HRT and breast cancer. That single study was enough to motivate quite a few women to swear off HRT, even though there have since been other studies that contradict the one done in Sweden.

The pharmaceutical companies used to assure us of the safety of estrogen when it is combined with progesterone (again, that's what HRT is). But, as a result of recent tests, those same drug companies are now busy reworking their formulas to reduce the breast cancer risk that they maintained wasn't there. It seems that estrogen does promote cell growth in the breasts.

Whoops.

It May Be the Whoops Factor

When I first started reading about what doctors and others are advising women about menopause, I was really glad I'm not a woman.

What hit me the hardest was what I have come to call "the Whoops Factor."

"Here, let us give you these pills," said the physicians of the 1970s.

Then, twenty years later, it was, "Whoops, we were wrong. Sorry, we didn't know the pills would cause cancer."

That wasn't just a small blunder.

Unfortunately, there have been a lot of whoopses in the area of women's health. In our lifetimes we have had the infamous Thalidomide and DES mistakes. Those drugs were supposed to counteract PMS and morning sickness, but instead caused women and their families untold misery.

We've also had a whoops or two in menopause medicine. ERT, before it became HRT, was one; needless hysterectomies were another.

As I said, I'm glad I'm not a woman.

It May Be That She Doesn't Want Any More Periods

Leaving behind their periods and paraphernalia is one of the things women like most about menopause. Because standardized HRT prescriptions mimic the premenopause levels of estrogen and progesterone pretty closely, HRT can keep the monthly blood flowing even though the ovaries are no longer launching eggs.

Many women don't ever start HRT, simply because they don't want to keep getting their period. And quite a few women who start HRT will stop because they don't want to have periods forever.

Fortunately, as the drug companies have gained experience with HRT, they've created formulations that can give women hormones without the continuing periods. It used to be that HRT was available in only a couple of basic dosages. Responding to the demand, drug companies are producing and doctors are prescribing a greater variety of dosages, some small enough to provide estrogen's benefits while minimizing the chances of causing continued menstrual bleeding.

It May Be That She Doesn't Want to Meddle With Nature

The women of our generation went back to natural childbirth and breast-feeding, and in the process took much more conscious and deliberate control of their reproductive lives than their mothers had. By experiencing childbirth as a natural process, female baby boomers have prepared themselves for the subsequent natural process of menopause.

Many of these women simply don't want to tamper with Mother Nature. These are the women who never start on HRT because they reason that keeping their periods going isn't normal, and that they shouldn't interfere with nature. They figure that nature, in its wisdom, created human menopause for a reason. They're not going to try to second-guess the natural order with prescribed drugs.

It May Be That She Views Menopause as a Natural Life Transition

Similarly, there are many women who feel that menopause is a natural life transition that should be honored, not treated as an illness. They look to other cultures and observe women undergoing little or no physical or emotional trauma during menopause. They then deduce that our cultural attitude is the chief culprit in our tendency to view menopause as a deficiency disease. They see women who are beyond childbearing age honored as elders, grandmothers, and wisdom figures in many societies, and they feel that these are the models they want to emulate.

It May Be That She Views It as a Growth Opportunity

Many of our spouses have been going to personal growth seminars for decades, sometimes dragging us men along, kicking and screaming. A lot of these women see menopause as a growth opportunity, and want to face the transition with their minds, bodies, and emotions unadulterated by drugs. They figure that there's a lot to learn, and they don't want to miss the insights and unfolding that can result from this life passage.

It May Be the Expense of Hormone Supplements

Only a small percentage of women who take HRT continue taking hormones for the rest of their lives; in fact, more than 75 percent stop at some point. Expense alone is a consideration, especially as people get older. HRT is not cheap, perhaps one reason that it is mostly taken by middle-class women.

So Should She Take HRT or Shouldn't She?

Certain women are medically advised against taking hormone supplementation. If your wife has had uterine, breast, cervical, or ovarian cancer, she is probably not a candidate for HRT. She may also be cautioned not to take hormones if she has a family history of cancer.

Certain other women are designated by doctors as being good candidates for HRT. If your wife's blood has a high count of LDL (the bad cholesterol), or if she has a family history of early heart attacks, she should consider estrogen for its potential benefits to her heart. The same is true if she is thought to be susceptible to osteoporosis (see Chapter Three for details). A woman may also consider herself a good candidate for hormone replenishment if hot flashes have left her feeling exhausted.

What's a Guy to Do?

Knowing all of the above, are you now wondering what you can do to help your wife make her thorny HRT decision, besides being an informed partner? Here's what I advise.

Number one: Try to listen. Be there for her as a pair of ears. She really may need to talk this one out.

The second thing she might want from you is support without judgment. This HRT decision is such a complex one that she may want to hear your opinion. But don't forget that an opinion is different from a pronouncement. Your offer of an opinion shouldn't end up making her feel pressured or judged.

What I mean is: what if she chooses something different from what you would choose for her? Will you hold it against her? Can you still support her?

My guess is that, in this tough area, support is what your wife may need more than anything else. Ask her how she wants support from you. Find out what you can do, both physically and emotionally. Please don't take my advice or anyone else's without asking *her*.

• • •

This is one area where I really wish I had done better. I assumed that I knew what my wife wanted from me as she was going through menopause—like a back rub, or help with shopping, or help around the house. Sometimes I got it right; Susan still remembers the time that I went to the market, bought a big hunk of filet mignon, and cooked it with mushrooms.

She did appreciate this kind of help, to be sure, but it took me quite a while to figure out what she really wanted. I could have discovered what she wanted way earlier if I'd just stopped and asked her. She would have told me. I still feel pretty dumb for missing something so obvious.

It turned out that, more than the occasional steak or back rub, Susan wanted emotional support. She wanted me to listen when she talked. She wanted my attention to be fully with her. She wanted me to be an aware partner and a support system. And she wanted me to understand the basis of her decisions and accept those decisions, whether or not I agreed with them.

Once she felt me to be understanding and informed, she was

much more open to hearing my thoughts and opinions. And when I was able to offer my opinions without trying to appear like an expert or authority, our discussions deepened to the point of being beneficial to our entire relationship.

Recommended Reading

It's easy to feel overloaded by the abundance of available information on menopause and HRT. But if you want to know more, let me suggest two books that are more evenhanded on the HRT subject than most. Each comes down on a different side of the issue. When you have read these for yourself, you may also want to share them with your wife, if she's open to reading them. But I'd be careful about telling her "You really ought to read this book." There's a big difference between sharing information and pressuring your wife to read what supports your point of view.

The Silent Passage: Menopause

The first book is by Gail Sheehy called *The Silent Passage: Menopause*. It's the book that first brought menopause into the public eye, and it's informative and easy to read. Sheehy relates the pros and cons of HRT through her own eyes, and details the making of her own difficult choice. The book is objective, and reads more like a memoir than a textbook, giving personal experience as well as facts and information.

Dr. Susan Love's Hormone Book: Making Informed Choices About Menopause

The second book, *Dr. Susan Love's Hormone Book* by Susan Love and Karen Lindsey, is also easy to read, even though it's more like a text. The book is complete and authoritative while being friendly and personal. The authors give a balanced overview, and their book is, in my opinion, the current ency-clopedia of menopause. It probably should be part of your family's permanent library.

A Reiteration of What You Shouldn't *Do*

As a man, you are able to stand back and look at menopause from a relatively detached place. After all, it's not your body. You may be able to see the hormone debate quite logically, carefully weigh all the pros and cons, and come up with some completely rational conclusion.

But your wife may *feel* something entirely different from what you have decided through your logical computations, and her intuition might count more to her than your mental reasoning. So be careful.

The number one no-no is trying to make her decision for her. This is definitely not a place for you to be forceful or judgmental.

There is almost universal agreement among the women I've talked to that they don't want you to try to take charge here. They are quite firm in their conviction that this is their decision. But, again, be available to listen, to talk, and to ask how you can be most helpful.

• • •

Many women, in fact most, do not want to take HRT but still want to do something to ease their menopause. In the next chapter, we'll look at some of the alternatives to HRT, both traditional and modern, that are now being made available to menopausal women. My guess is that your wife may already have tried a few.

Alternatives to HRT

I sn't it odd that the measures taken by the vast majority of the world's women in response to menopause are labeled "alternatives," as if somehow these measures are out of the mainstream?

Only about one quarter of menopausal women in the United States take hormone replacement therapy, and even fewer women in other countries. That works out to fewer than 5 percent of menopausal women worldwide who are on HRT. So why don't hormones get called "the alternative"?

The Most Common Options

Throughout the world, without question, the most widely chosen alternative treatment for menopause is no treatment. The only thing that the majority of women do about menopause is go through it.

After no treatment at all, traditional approaches that make use of native plants and natural medicines are the second most popular alternative.

In this country, one important outgrowth of traditional or natural approaches to menopause is an emerging alternative to HRT called natural hormone replacement (NHR). As I'll detail a little later in this chapter, if a woman and her doctor feel uncomfortable about HRT because the drugs don't duplicate nature, but they still want to replace the hormones in the woman's system, they now can.

There are yet other alternative approaches to menopause that are gaining popularity. These are the various psychological and spiritual practices such as meditation, support groups, and rite of passage ceremonies. In Chapter Ten, "Passages and Paradigm Shifts," I'll discuss some of them.

Traditional Approaches

For literally thousands of years in some cultures, healers have been using native plants and medicines to smooth the menopausal transition. Many American women, along with those individuals in the medical profession who are more holistically inclined, are now discovering alternatives to HRT such as Chinese herbs, acupuncture, Western herbs and vitamins, and creams made of wild yams from Mexico.

Herbs, Vitamins, and Minerals

Worldwide, of those women who do something besides "just go through" menopause, more take herbs than any other remedy. While hormones are beginning to make inroads, traditional medicines are still the most widely prescribed treatment.

Even in the West, it's generally known that, because of our diet, stressful lifestyle, and environmental pollution, vitamin and mineral supplements are a good idea. There is even wide agreement in the medical community that supplements of the B vitamins, vitamin D, calcium, and magnesium are needed by the menopausal woman.

Herbs are also beginning to gain greater acceptance. Seeing an obvious opportunity, herb producers are responding. You can tell how well menopause herbs are selling by noticing all the formulas that are now available, not only in health food stores but through supermarkets and drugstore chains as well. If you're seeing herbs like black cohosh, primrose, and Dong Quai around your house, probably your wife has already started on an herbal regimen.

While a lot of helpful herbs are available, there are fewer good herbalists. Fortunately, a growing number of osteopaths, naturopaths, chiropractors, acupuncturists, and even ground-breaking M.D.s are gaining the knowledge and expertise to accurately prescribe the herbs that a woman may need.

Maybe the biggest help you can offer your wife here is to make sure that she isn't heedlessly heading out to the health food store and stocking up on a dozen or more kinds of supplements. Herbs are powerful medicines, so caution in their use is wise.

Countless books on herbs are available, but most of these are not specifically written to the needs of menopausal women. Two books that I can recommend in this area are (again) *Dr. Susan Love's Hormone Book* and *Menopausal Years: The Wise Woman's Way*, by Susun Weed. As I have said, Dr. Love's book is encyclopedic in all areas of menopause; it includes an excellent and comprehensive section on herbs. Susun Weed is an herbalist with decades of experience who has written the first herb book specifically tailored to show how herbs can help during menopause.

Chinese Herbs, Eastern Medicine, and Acupuncture

What may be even more effective than Western herbs is a branch of herbal medicine that can broadly be called "Chinese herbs." If they work better than Western herbs, it's probably because Eastern healers have been using herbs continuously for thousands of years.

Because the Eastern approach to health is to balance the entire body, Chinese herbs are given as part of a program that often includes acupuncture, supplements, meditation, and some form of physical exercise—possibly even yoga. While effective, this regimen offers no quick fix for the menopausal woman, although some women do get relatively fast improvement where their hot flashes, mood swings, and energy level are concerned.

When acupuncture and Eastern medicine are used during menopause, the regimen usually includes dietary prescriptions and proscriptions as well. If your wife stops eating dairy products and cold foods and eats more brown rice and veggies, and if a few times a day she takes a handful of herbs she didn't get from the health food store, she's probably on this program.

Over the last couple of decades, acupuncture has become widely accepted in the United States as an effective treatment for pain—so effective that many Western M.D.s are going back to school to learn the basics of this Asian treatment. As of this writing, there are more than thirty schools and colleges of acupuncture in the U.S., and more than twenty states certify and license acupuncturists. Insurance companies are even starting to pay for acupuncture treatments.

Acupuncture works on the idea that the body's life force travels along certain lines, or meridians. The acupuncturist is trained to locate these meridians, as well as the particular points along them that, when stimulated, can help heal various parts of the body. Acupuncturists use extremely thin, disposable needles to stimulate the points. Occasionally these hair-like needles sting a little when they are inserted, but they are tapped in shallowly and mostly they aren't even felt. Depending on the practitioner, the needles can be left in for a few minutes or for as long as an hour.

I don't know of any negative side effects to Eastern medicine, as long as you go to someone who has been well trained. If your state licenses acupuncturists, you can call your state department of health for a listing of qualified practitioners. If your state doesn't license acupuncturists, call the National Commission for the Certification of Acupuncturists at (202) 232-1404 for a referral.

Practitioners of acupuncture don't always practice Chinese medicine, but most practitioners of Chinese medicine are acupuncturists. I would recommend that your wife consider seeing someone who has received schooling and training in both disciplines. A qualified acupuncturist who is nationally certified will be able to use Dipl.Ac. (for Diplomate of Acupuncture) after his or her name, and many who are trained in Oriental medicine call themselves O.M.D.s. A reputable and professional acupuncturist in the U.S. should also belong to one or more of the local and national professional associations.

A qualified acupuncturist should be able to do more than insert needles and prescribe herbs. As is the case with any health practitioner, proper diagnosis is absolutely essential to proper treatment. If your wife is incompletely or improperly diagnosed, important problems can be left untreated. Reputable colleges of Chinese medicine include comprehensive courses of study in diagnosis. One way to find out if your wife's potential acupuncturist has been thoroughly trained is if he or she is able to give your wife a traditional written diagnosis.

But in many cases, the biggest roadblock to your wife receiving the benefits of Chinese medicine has nothing to do with the practitioner. *You* might be the problem. Unfortunately, acupuncture still raises eyebrows among the uninformed.

• • •

I know. I was guilty of skepticism until just a couple of years ago. I was lucky, though, because I got my introduction to acupuncture through my regular doctor.

In another example of questionable "wonder drug wisdom," during high school and college I received countless cortisone injections into my shoulders to help me extend my swimming career. As a result, for the last thirty years I've lived with a constant nagging pain because I have no cartilage in either shoulder. Western medicine offered no relief outside of painkillers or shoulder replacements—neither of which my doctor recommended in my case. So she referred me to an acupuncturist.

Figuring I had nothing to lose except maybe a few bucks, I

took her advice and saw a traditional Korean practitioner for a few months. I must admit that the pincushion effect wasn't entirely painless, but it wasn't bad. And, lo and behold—it worked. After only a couple months of treatments, I was pain free for the first time in thirty years. As a result of this experience, I'm a believer.

So I recommend that, if your skepticism has kept your wife from the potential relief that acupuncture can provide, you step back a few paces, withhold your judgments, and support her in getting a course of acupuncture treatments if she wants to. Chinese medicine has helped millions and millions of women over the centuries. You and your mate will very likely be pleasantly surprised.

Natural Hormones

Many women would love to replace their lost hormones if they could do it naturally—that is, with hormones that exactly duplicate what the body of a human female produces. The hormones offered in HRT are either synthetic chemicals or are what a female *horse* makes. Fortunately for the women who want natural hormones, these are becoming available.

But what is a *natural* hormone?

Not surprisingly, there's not a lot of agreement on the subject. When we think of "natural food," we might picture crunchy granola, a bunch of organic carrots with their tops still on, or some nutritious whole-grain bread . . . in other words, food that is unrefined or as close to its natural state as possible. The one area of agreement around natural hormone replacement is that this is *not* the way natural hormones are defined. All "natural" hormones have been significantly modified from their natural state.

The most commonly used definition is this: a natural hormone is one that is molecularly identical to a human hormone. *Identical-to-human* means *identical-to-nature*, which also means *unpatentable*. Therefore, natural hormones are not now available from the pharmaceutical companies that equate patentable drugs with profitable drugs. Which means that, at this point, natural hormones are hardly available at all. But the demand for natural hormones is growing, and so as surely as night follows the day, the supply will grow as well.

Natural Progesterone

When a woman goes through menopause, her estrogen output decreases by about 60 percent. Although her ovaries now produce much less estrogen, they do continue to produce some, and her fat cells and adrenal glands produce some as well. But her progesterone level drops by more than 95 percent. The ovaries stop producing all but a tiny amount, and there is no other part of the body that produces progesterone.

In the early days of hormone replacement therapy, only estrogen was thought to be important to replace in a menopausal woman. After the uterine cancer scare, doctors began opposing estrogen with progesterone. But they saw no intrinsic benefit in the progesterone; it was used just to counterbalance estrogen's risks.

But menopausal women have used progesterone in various natural forms for hundreds, or maybe thousands, of years. Without knowing that all yams contain a powerful progesterone precursor (a precursor is a molecule that the body can make into something else, in this case progesterone), Native American healers have been treating menopausal women with various wild yam remedies for centuries.

Only recently have doctors discovered progesterone's intrinsic value. As with many a medical discovery, good luck and good guessing played an important part in the story. Dr. John R. Lee, widely recognized as one of the pioneers in this area of expertise, first prescribed natural progesterone on a hope and a hunch. In the 1970s, when estrogen was still being prescribed unopposed by progesterone, Lee found that some of his patients could not tolerate estrogen at all. He had heard of a cosmetic cream that contained progesterone from wild yams that could be used for estrogen opposition. When he recommended to his estrogen-intolerant patients that they try the cream by itself, he was amazed at the results. Progesterone showed promising results not only with hot flashes, but also with osteoporosis.

Doctors and scientists in the U.S., Europe, and Canada have expanded on Dr. Lee's work by conducting intriguing and encouraging research that shows that natural progesterone may be even better at stopping osteoporosis than is estrogen, which only temporarily slows bone loss. These studies have shown that natural progesterone actually produces an *increase* in bone density—something estrogen can't do.

Other preliminary studies show promise that natural progesterone may even help counter heart disease and breast cancer. Women also report the welcome side effects of fewer mood swings, fewer hot flashes, and more energy when they take natural progesterone.

Another intrinsic benefit of natural progesterone is that it is a precursor to estrogen and other hormones. In other words, when a woman has more than enough progesterone, her body can take any excess of the precursor and transform it into the estrogen that she needs. Some aware physicians are using this knowledge to decrease the amounts of estrogen they're prescribing to women who show an intolerance to it. These doctors realize that a woman's body, by using its instinctive wisdom, will manufacture the needed amount of estrogen from the progesterone.

As a result of Dr. Lee's and others' work, there is a growing demand for natural progesterone. Many formulations are available, mostly in cream form and mostly from health food stores. Your wife has probably heard of wild yam, and has maybe even tried one or more of the creams.

You might be able to help her here. Some creams contain nothing more than ground-up wild yams. To be helpful, the yams need to be refined so that the progesterone precursor, diosgenin (also found in soybeans), is isolated and refined into progesterone that can be readily used by the body.

When diosgenin is converted to natural progesterone in a laboratory, the resulting creams are powerful medicine. The best compounds are made to standard strengths so that women know how much they are taking. Dr. Lee's wonderfully thorough and informative book, *What Your Doctor May Not Tell You about Menopause*, contains tables on pages 271 and 334 to 335 that list various brand-name progesterone creams and the amounts of progesterone they actually contain.

Natural Hormone Replacement (NHR)

Natural progesterone is also available in prescription-strength formulations. In this form, a doctor most often prescribes it in combination with other natural hormones. This complete program is known as natural hormone replacement or NHR. (Actually, natural hormone replacement is so new that the various experts haven't yet agreed on an acronym. Some call it NHT for natural hormone therapy and some refer to natural hormones simply as "the naturals.")

Besides progesterone, humans make estrogen, testosterone, and the multihormone precursor called DHEA. In fact, a woman's body makes three kinds of estrogens: estriol, estradiol, and estrone. About 60 to 80 percent of what a woman makes is estriol, with estradiol and estrone splitting the other 20 to 40 percent evenly. When doctors prescribe NHR, they will prescribe hormones that not only match the molecular structure of these human estrogens, but match these naturally occurring percentages as well.

By contrast, Premarin, the estrogen usually prescribed in HRT, is made from the urine of pregnant mares (hence the name, Pre-mar-in). It provides estrone almost exclusively, with just a little touch of estradiol.

Why should this be of any concern? Well, some women want to do things as close to nature's way as possible, and some doctors feel this natural approach is important because of the past "whoopses" that have accompanied HRT.

If your wife is one of the growing number of women who want NHR, she'll probably have to search for a doctor to work with her. I suggest finding a naturopath or calling ACAM (the American College for the Advancement of Medicine, at (800) 532-3688). All of these doctors have at least been exposed to the ideas of NHR, and many are avid practitioners.

All natural estrogens and progesterones are made from the hormone precursors found in soybeans and wild Mexican yams. Since they are not patentable drugs offered in standardized formulations by drug companies, the prescriptions will need to be made from scratch by a pharmacist, just like in the old days. These kinds of druggists, called compounding pharmacists, almost disappeared in the last few decades, but they're making a comeback. They even have two associations that can give you referrals: The International Academy of Compounding Pharmacists (IACP) at (800) 927-4227, and the Professional Compounding Centers of America (PCCA) at (800) 331-2498.

I know of two pharmacies that specialize in compounds for women: Madison Pharmacy in Wisconsin, at (608) 833-9102; and the Women's International Pharmacy in Wisconsin and Arizona, at (800) 279-5708. Your wife's doctor can work with them directly even if you live in a different area. If you want to find a local doctor who works with NHR, you can call them and they'll be glad to try to help.

The first book I found on natural hormone replacement therapy is by one of natural hormone replacement's primary founders, Jonathan V. Wright, M.D., along with John Morgenthaler. This informative and easy to read book is called *Natural Hormone Replacement for Women Over 45*. Another book I recommend is *Natural Woman, Natural Menopause*, by Marcus Laux, N.D., and Christine Conrad. Don't be confused by terminology; Laux and Conrad use the term "the naturals" where Wright and Morgenthaler use "NHR."

Are There Any NHR Side Effects?

Although the jury is still out, preliminary data suggest that the natural kinds of estrogens and progesterone don't have the undesirable side effects of their manufactured cousins.

But caution is always a good idea with drugs. Even some vitamins and herbs can be harmful if you take too high a dosage. And natural hormones are extremely powerful, even in minute amounts. A good NHR doctor will take extensive blood, saliva, or urine tests and will have a long consultation with your wife before working with a compounding pharmacist to make up an individualized prescription. And he or she will follow up with more tests and consultations and adjustments, to make sure that the hormones are doing what they should.

As a matter of fact, it is normal for a lot of women who don't want to use HRT to approach natural hormones slowly, and only if the other alternatives don't give satisfactory results. Quite often a woman will have tried herbs and vitamins or acupuncture before she tries any kind of hormone. Remember, hormones are powerful drugs.

Some women object to NHR simply because it is a hormone replacement. They figure that if nature takes the hormones away, humans shouldn't be so presumptuous as to think they should replace them. I must admit that I shared this view before I started writing this book. But I've come to understand and accept that some women are greatly affected by menopause and really do want to "get their lives back." After learning enough to develop some compassion for these women, I have dropped my judgments.

• • •

And it's a good thing that I have, because—after five years of going through the various stages of menopause while trying every alternative available—my wife has had enough.

Susan has never wanted to use conventional HRT. As she says, "It just doesn't feel right to me." But she has had continuous hot flashes and night sweats that have not only caused her to buy a new wardrobe—cardigans and zip-ups instead of pullovers—but have also robbed her of her energy. She's been subject to moodiness, forgetfulness, and even some mild depression. She's tried Western herbs, Chinese herbs, exercise, nutrition, acupuncture, and attitude adjustments. She's read all the books, has talked with her sister and friends, and has dealt quite well with the changing of the "mom role" and the onset of the empty nest.

And she's still wiped out.

When Susan first heard about natural hormones, she was cautious, wondering if she should second-guess nature. She held off starting NHR because she honors menopause as nature's way and sees it as part of a natural transition to a "wise woman" stage of life.

But she dearly wants her energy back.

We talked about natural hormones at great length. I tried to put myself in the supportive and listening mode, and the more I listened the more I realized I wanted her to get whatever relief she can get. She's put the best possible face on menopause, but it's been damnably hard. I want her to feel better.

After finding out as much as she could, Susan finally decided that the natural way felt sufficiently safe. So she started NHR.

And I'm really glad.

She began by using a natural progesterone cream called Progest and got some relief from her hot flashes. They didn't go away, but they came less frequently and were less intense. But while the brand-name progesterone cream has helped, her energy was still low. So she found a holistic M.D. who has helped her even more by working with a compounding pharmacist to prescribe prescription-grade natural progesterone in capsules and cream, as well as all three kinds of natural estrogen. Most importantly, they're making sure that Susan gets the hormones in the ratios and percentages that her body needs— the ones in which nature provides them.

As I write this, we are still only a month or so into the new regimen. While there has been further improvement, Susan is still not all the way to where she wants to be. She and her doctor and the pharmacist are adjusting her prescription to her needs, which is a normal part of the process. From what we understand, it could take as long as a year to get the prescription just right.

I'll keep you posted in future editions.

10
$\mathscr{P}$assages and Paradigm Shifts

W omen are lucky to go through menopause." When- ever that viewpoint is held (and I have heard this idea expressed), it is because menopause is being seen as an initiatory passage, a time when a woman moves from one distinct stage of her life to another. The process is similar to when she moved from childhood into puberty.

Feminine Transitions

In their life cycles, women move through several distinct passages: menstruation, motherhood, and menopause. Not all women participate in motherhood, but, if she menstruates, a woman will go through menopause. During each of these passages, an old part of her passes away and a new part is born. This kind of metamorphosis is never a comfortable process.

Menopause is a time of transformation, and—in the physical sense, at least—it's not an option. As Germaine Greer says in her book *The Change: Women, Aging, and the Menopause*, "The fifty-year-old woman has no option but to register the great change that is taking place within her . . . . "

Menopause can be a time imbued with meaning, but in our society it's usually not. It can signify the end of the childbearing season and the beginning of a time of wisdom and contribution.

Menopause might even be celebrated, but too often just the opposite is true.

Greer continues, "There is no rite of passage to surround the middle-aged woman with solemnity, no seclusion ordered for her, no special period of rest. She cannot withdraw to a menopause hut and sit and talk with other menopausal women."

Virtually all societies have rituals and ceremonies for important passages. In many ancient societies, when children became adults they went through rituals such as vision quests and walkabouts, ceremonies in which the adolescent walked for days in solitude or fasted alone in the wilderness, hoping to receive a vision about his or her future as an adult. There were special ceremonial centers: temples, kivas, pyramids, and sacred mounds.

Modern societies still celebrate important life events and passages with countless feasts, festivals, saint's days, confirmations, bar and bat mitzvahs, and the like.

Unfortunately, menopause isn't included on that list. Instead, the passage is too often surrounded by silence, shame, and fear of the loss of youth and fertility. Only recently has this been changing.

Mentors and Guides

Traditional societies had the wisdom to anoint guides and mentors to help people through difficult passages.

In our society, we still do some mentoring. At puberty, a girl usually gets advice and explanations from her mother. She needs a woman's experience in order to understand about this first blood flowing out of her body, and if she has been prepared in advance she's less likely to find her first menstruation frightening or embarrassing. Also, our generation has brought about a return to the practice of midwifery, to give assistance during pregnancy and in the birthing process. Often, too, mothers still help their daughters learn to care for their newborns.

But there's been no parallel help with menopause. Up until 1991, when the life-passages expert Gail Sheehy published her silence-breaking book, *The Silent Passage: Menopause*, the subject was usually addressed (if it was mentioned at all) in hushed tones. Thanks to Sheehy and others, this phase of life is now getting the public discussion that it warrants. In the last seven years, more than two hundred fifty books on the subject have been published.

Also, a growing network now exists of menopausal mentors who offer commonsense help. This support system is probably most needed in the early, mystifying stages of menopause when a woman hasn't quite figured out what's going on. Just to know that there are other women out there who can provide guidance through the maze of menopause can be deeply reassuring.

Mentors can be found through friends, newsletters, or menopause centers; through the grapevine, over the Internet, or through national and regional groups; or even by placing a personal notice in your local newspaper. As more and more baby boomers come of age, these support systems should only continue to grow.

Hey, who knows? Maybe some day there'll be a network for menopausal husbands.

The Grandmother Hypothesis

Humans are the only animals that experience menopause. There has to be a reason why, out of all of creation, only human females outlive their reproductive time.

Sociologists, anthropologists, and evolutionary biologists theorize that menopause has evolved for some very good reasons—their theory is called "the Grandmother Hypothesis." First of all, they suggest that because human children take so many years to mature, our species needs caring elders to help bear the physical burden of child care. We are not hatched out of eggs and left to fend for ourselves. We need many years of protection and instruction before we can even manage to find our own food.

And it is not just physical help that grandmothers can provide. Because our social organization is so complex, female elders may also have evolved because they are needed to help teach the necessary moral and spiritual lessons.

Wise women have formed the spiritual core of countless societies, passing on wisdom and tradition while they literally helped keep their families alive. The grandmother hypothesis in its fullness suggests that elder women evolved not only for the biological survival of our species, but also for the spiritual well-being of humanity. Where would we be without our feminine elders?

While our culture belittles the aged of both genders and consigns them to nursing homes, many cultures both modern and traditional have venerated older females as elders, allowing them at menopause to step free of certain taboos. For instance, in Papua New Guinea and prerevolution China, elder women were liberated from the power of their husbands. In the South Pacific, elder women initiated adolescent males into the wonders of sex. After menopause, Rajput women in India can leave the women's quarters, unveil, and talk and drink with men. In Bali, they can use explicit language along with the men. In Micronesia they can become healers. And in Ethiopia they can walk where only men could before.

Postmenopausal women of the Crow Nation become the Keepers of the Law, specifically the Law of Good Relationships; Winnebago elder women can help build ceremonial lodges; mature female Afghanis can smoke tobacco and drink alcohol; elder women in Mozambique are freed from dietary restrictions; and in Mexico and the Cree Nation of Canada they can become a shaman or a priestess.

Regardless of the culture, grandmothers are a wonderful and necessary part of society. We are ignoring an essential resource by dismissing them to the "bone heap." But fortunately, things are changing.

Women are reawakening to their postmenopausal potential. Since so many of them no longer define themselves solely as bearers of children, they don't see themselves as somehow less because of menopause. They see menopause not as a sickness, but as an important, even essential, transformation into a time of deepened meaning and purpose in their lives.

Transformations

Perhaps this paradigm shift is happening because women are indignant about the degrading views our culture has held of menopause, as characterized by Freud's description of the menopausal woman as "quarrelsome and obstinate, petty and stingy, sadistic, and anal erotic."

The difference between looking at menopause as a disease or as a transformation is the difference between night and day. After reading Susun Weed's *Menopausal Years: The Wise Woman Way*, a book devoted to honoring menopause, my wife and I could understand that the painful process of menopause is a necessary part of the whole of her life. Another good book of essays and interviews dedicated to looking at menopause as a transition and a transformation is *Red Moon Passage: The Power and Wisdom of Menopause* by Bonnie Horrigan.

Menopause is not only about endings. During any personal transformation, there is pain as old parts of the self pass away. But the pain is bearable, or even welcome, if one sees the process as beneficial, as bringing new potential.

The term "wisdom years" is getting tossed around a lot lately, as are phrases like "postmenopausal zest" and "optimistic, can-do stage of life." Don't be surprised if you see your wife adopting these attitudes. A self long buried might be waiting to arise within her and transform her life in meaningful ways.

Many women at midlife are discovering new careers or reenergizing old ones. Some women are starting businesses; some are becoming the artists they always wanted to be; others get involved in service projects; others go back to school for that degree they wanted but never had time to pursue.

As I pointed out near the end of Chapter Six, many women feel that the upheavals of menopause provide an excellent opportunity for emotional deepening. While the issues that arise may not be easy to deal with, these women are glad that menopause has given them a chance to see the patterns of their lives and to work on completing them.

Other women are finding a deepening spirituality. Look around at virtually any spiritual gathering these days. The vast majority of attendees are women, and a surprising number are older. Maybe the elder women of the world are answering an inner prompting to do something about the spiritual emptiness of our materialistic society.

Maybe they will get us headed back in the right direction.

Increasingly, as ideas about menopause as an important passage are entering the culture, more and more women are adopting this more enlightened view. Be prepared to observe your partner finding menopause to be a time for personal reflection and growth, a time for developing a new sense of self.

Unfortunately, many women, overburdened with work and domestic responsibilities, and possibly with the care of their aging parents, feel that they don't have time for introspection. If a woman doesn't get any time to herself, it's harder for her to experience menopause as a positive transformation.

You can help a lot by understanding and honoring your wife's need for time to slow down, to take care of her inner needs, to recharge by spending quiet moments alone, and to reevaluate what's important to her. As well as being understanding, you should make extra sure that you carry your share of domestic and care-giving responsibilities.

You will be richly rewarded. When your partner's life is more balanced and is growing in the direction she wants, she can bring enrichment rather than stress to your relationship.

• • •

But seeing midlife as a transformation is not just something for women to do. Many authors, therapists, and specialists in personal growth suggest that men might want to look at it that way, too.

Like our wives, we men too often see increasing age as the road to oblivion. But it's not; midlife is only a passage from one productive phase of life to another. In the next chapter, we'll take a look at some of the ways we men are affected at this stage of the game. Lately the term "male menopause" has been entering the vernacular. Can this be a valid term?

11 Men and Midlife

I s there a male menopause? Technically, of course, since men don't menstruate, there can be no such thing. But, like women, we men feel a barrage of physical effects at midlife, due to a decrease in certain hormones. What this means is that your declining sexuality, for instance, is not all in your head. Just like women, we go through changes that are partly psychological—what we commonly call "the midlife crisis."

Physical Changes That Men Go Through

Hormones and Sex

As I said before, our testosterone peaked when we were adolescents. No question about it, we were at the mercy of our hormones there for a while. Our minds were consumed by sexual thoughts and fantasies, and parts of our bodies responded mysteriously.

Somewhere around forty or so you may have noticed testosterone's slow ebb. You might have missed an orgasm, or not been able to have sex twice in a row. That book title about "multiple male orgasms" might have caught your eye.

Losing our sexual urgency is a natural part of aging. Since it's going to happen, we need to get used to the idea.

Hormones and Aging

Testosterone is not the only hormone we lose over time; there's a long list of others. While they are not as well publicized, there are even hormone replacement therapies for men now, too. Some are available from doctors and some from health food stores. (Do you remember the DHEA publicity?) If you are interested in the details of our hormonal changes, I suggest Jed Diamond's comprehensive book, *Male Menopause*. Diamond makes sense out of what in Europe has long been called "andropause" or "viropause," terms better suited than menopause for what happens hormonally to men during their middle years.

It has long been well documented that men go through more than just sexual changes at midlife. Some of the physical changes we might experience are weight gain, memory loss, bone thinning, diminished strength and endurance, and deteriorating eyesight.

If you add going bald and getting gray hair, these would sound just like the signs of getting old. That's because these *are* the signs of getting old. Researchers suspect that these effects might be caused by the reductions in our hormones, because when men are given hormone supplements some of these indicators of aging can be stopped or even reversed.

• • •

"Take hormones."

"Feel younger."

"*Look* younger."

When I first thought about feeling and looking younger, I must say I was tempted.

"Wouldn't that be cool?" I thought. "More energy. I'd sure like that. Maybe I should get some of those pills."

Then I thought about the possible side effects. An increased risk of prostate cancer is one. And then I remembered the advice I've been so freely dispensing throughout this book, about the acceptance of aging. I must admit that I fight that one pretty hard. I don't like getting old either.

In time I realized that these thoughts must be somewhat similar to what my wife goes through. And, with this last realization, I had my first breath of real compassion for what women face in their decisions about HRT. I finally understood.

Psychological Issues of the Midlife Crisis

"Andropausal" men not only go through physical changes; there are psychological issues we must face as well. *Male Menopause* details quite a list. Let me mention a few that I think tend to define the midlife crisis.

- You might want to deny that you're getting older.
- You could lose your self-confidence or self-esteem.
- You might not even know who you are at times, as if you've lost your identity.
- You might experience a sense of your life losing its meaning or purpose.

Denial or Acceptance?

When we men enter midlife, the first issue a lot of us will face is how hard it is to accept losing our youth. We lose our accustomed outer identity just as much as women do. No one remains young, buff, and twenty-five forever.

Humans are pretty good at denial. Some part of us likes to think we stay attractive as we get old and fat. We can even lie to ourselves when we look in the mirror, sucking in that gut unconsciously.

But another part of us knows. We can't fool ourselves all of the time.

Still, we'd like to.

That beautiful woman who pays attention to you for whatever reason can deepen your denial. It can be reassuring to a part of your middle-aged psyche to feel that a younger woman is attracted to you.

• • •

Virtually every week for the past six years, I've led seminars for Stephen Covey based on his book *The Seven Habits of Highly Effective People.* In a recent course, one of the participants was a drop-dead gorgeous blue-eyed blond—young, well-dressed, and with a beautiful figure. As I presented the course, her eyes followed me around the room like I was a moving target.

In the evenings I like to work out in the hotel exercise room. Sure enough, the first night she was there, looking altogether too good in her tights and tank top. She hung around after she was done with her workout, stretching like a cat on her towel, directly in my line of sight.

When I finally finished up and was toweling off my sweat, she asked me out to dinner.

You have to know that I'd just grown a beard, the first one since I was a hippie. Only this time it came out gray. A part of me had been worrying that it made me look old. And I'd recently expanded a pants size, so I was working out extra hard.

To put it bluntly, I was feeling old and fat.

But getting asked out by a beautiful young woman made me feel pretty much like a colt. I liked it. Her attention stroked a part of my ego that I hadn't known needed stroking. It sure felt good. There was even a momentary rush of temptation. Testosterone has no conscience, you know.

But I do. Fortunately, I'd long since decided I was never going to fall for that trap and do something stupid to destroy my marriage.

I enjoyed my dinner alone.

Self-Esteem or Other-Esteem?

Self-esteem that depends on outside approval is illusory, because it comes from someone or something other than us. When our worth originates from anywhere but our self, it can't be "self" worth. It isn't self-esteem, but other-esteem.

Yet, to a certain extent, we all gain some sense of self, or identity, from outer things . . . maybe from how we look, from our possessions, from our role at work, from our past accomplishments—or even from some young blond. However, when we become dependent on job titles, appearances, or others' opinions as the determinants of how we feel about ourselves, we give those outer things great power over us and rob ourselves of our intrinsic power and security.

Then, when the job title or the good looks leave us, we can be in for a rough ride.

New Roles, Appearances, and Identities

Do the changes brought by midlife mean that you could be in for a new identity? Well, if not a whole new identity, then at least a new exterior. You are losing your youth, and maybe getting paunchy and gray and wrinkled like me.

But, more than outer appearances, some of us are losing an old and familiar sense of self. Our trim, fit self has always signified someone young and vital, someone in the hunt for the prize. Our gray, flabby self could mean that we are soon to be out of the hunt—retired, consigned to the golf course, and suddenly inconsequential in the grand scheme of things. At this stage of life, it can help to have a deeper sense of self . . . one that comes not from the outside, but from the inside.

The transitions of midlife often change not only our appearance, but also our roles. The angst that often comes along with this is not bad or wrong; it is to be expected.

Carl Jung, the great Swiss psychologist, maintained that

midlife upheavals are normal. He pointed out that middle age is a natural time of transition from the first half of life, which was perhaps filled with accomplishment and acquisition, to a second half that might be characterized more by introspection and acceptance.

Jung even predicted, in a way, the modern midlife crisis when he taught that previously unknown parts of ourselves might struggle to ascend to new prominence, parts that were hitherto "inferior functions" or even opposite aspects of ourselves. For example, in the first half of life we might have been concerned about how much we could create and acquire, whereas, at midlife, we might start to be more concerned about the legacy we will leave for others.

Jung suggested that we would feel a natural "tension of the opposites" as these internal transformations tried to take place. A normal tendency for most of us is not to "sit with" or accept the potentially transformative tension; we'd rather ignore it and try to remain the same good old boy. Regardless, our souls are yearning to grow, to become more. If we are to be transformed into the elders we are supposed to become, there will always be some tension.

Often the tension is revealed when we ask ourselves midlife-crisis questions such as: "Is this all there is?" or "Is this all that life is about?"

According to Jung, the answer is: "No, there's more."

From Self-Actualization to Self-Transcendence

The American psychologist Abraham Maslow gave us a clue as to what Jung's "more" might be. Maslow noted two important concepts about human needs and motivation:

First, only unfulfilled needs motivate us. That is, if you are starving there is nothing more important to you than food. Conversely, once your hunger has been filled, you are no longer motivated to eat.

Second, needs are arranged hierarchically, with the lower

needs always taking precedence when they are unfulfilled. That is, you will take care of your survival needs before you will attend to your need to feel good about yourself or your need to leave a legacy to society.

When Maslow originally laid out his ascending list of needs—his famous "hierarchy of needs"—he placed "self-actualization" at the top. The self-actualized man, for instance, is one who has reached his full potential, becoming all that he can be. Jung would say that this is what the first half of our life is supposed to be about.

Maslow, toward the end of his life, and perhaps as a result of his own midlife realizations, capped his pyramid with another need: "self-transcendence," or the need to feel and know ourselves to be part of something bigger than ourselves.

When we've taken care of our self-actualization needs, Maslow taught, we no longer gain motivation and fulfillment from developing our egos. Life becomes more about leaving a legacy, or making a difference, or giving back. So Ted Turner, in the second half of his life, gives away a billion. But Bill Gates, in the first half of his, is still accumulating.

(Interestingly, women have pointed out that Maslow's hierarchy is based on male experience and that it describes men better than it describes women. Child-rearing—perhaps our most basic example of human self-transcendence—occupies the first half of a woman's life. The full reaching of her potential, or her self-actualization, may not come until the second half of life—when she goes back to school, develops a career, and so forth. Women have understood and filled the need to be a part of something more than themselves all along. The first half of their lives is often primarily about connectedness and community, with self-actualization coming in a distant second.)

Meaning and Purpose

One of the challenges of the transition into the second half of life is finding where we will now get our sense of meaning and purpose. What was meaningful to us before, like money or climbing the ladder of success, may no longer be so important. If we are not prepared for this change, we can find ourselves in a spiritual void, with potentially serious consequences.

When I lead "Seven Habits" seminars, I usually ask the participants how many of them know of someone who died shortly after retirement or after his or her spouse died. Usually far more than half the hands go up. Apparently, when our jobs or spouses contain so much meaning, to the point of becoming our identity, we can feel so empty when they are gone that we can actually die.

The work of Hans Selye and Viktor Frankl regarding the importance of meaning can be very helpful in understanding why this happens. Frankl, a survivor of the Nazi death camps, built an effective school of psychotherapy around the idea that keeping meaning in our lives makes us physically, mentally, emotionally, and spiritually healthy.

He noticed that, even in the hell of Auschwitz, some of his fellow prisoners could find some purpose to their day. In his extraordinary book, *Man's Search for Meaning: An Introduction to Logotherapy*, Frankl wrote: "We who lived in concentration camps can remember the men who walked throughout the huts comforting others, giving away their last piece of bread . . . ." These people, he said, found meaning, perhaps even joy, in their lives in the camps.

"There is nothing in the world," Frankl continued, ". . . that would so effectively help one to survive even the worst conditions as the knowledge that there is a meaning in one's life. There is much wisdom in the words of Nietzsche: 'He who has a *why* to live for can bear almost any *how*.'"

Frankl taught that meaning, or "a why to live for," could make the difference between life and death; it was the prisoners who found this meaning that survived. Jung voiced these thoughts when he said, "Meaninglessness is illness." In other words, meaning promotes life and the lack of meaning undermines it.

Frankl further taught that "man's search for meaning may

arouse inner tension rather than inner equilibrium. . . . Such tension is an indispensable prerequisite of mental health."

Thankfully, most of us will never face tension as extreme as what Frankl experienced at the hands of the Nazis. The worst stress that we will ordinarily deal with is the tension of daily life. According to Hans Selye, the great Canadian sociologist who conducted seminal research on stress, when we have stress without meaning, or "distress" in his terminology, our immune systems are weakened.

Selye found another kind of stress that he named "eustress," or good stress. What makes the distinction between distress and eustress is meaning, "working for ends that give lasting results that you consider worthwhile." In his book *The Stress of Life*, he exhorts us to "use [our] innate capacities to enjoy the eustress of fulfillment . . . to fight and work for some goal [we] consider worthwhile."

Agreeing with Frankl and Jung, Selye taught that, instead of sapping our energy, eustress promotes mental health. He found that it even strengthens our immune system and adds years to our lives.

You may have felt this kind of meaningful stress when you've been absorbed in an important project, or perhaps at a time when you've been motivated to learn something significant for your career, or when you've been working toward a challenging goal that you had decided you strongly wanted to achieve. On its way to making us healthy, this kind of "stress" creates energy, excitement, enthusiasm, and—most importantly—fulfillment.

Living a meaningful life is always a source of fulfillment. Yet, as we move into midlife, what we derive meaning from can change with our new "identity." For so many of us, the big question becomes: "So what is the rest of my life going to be about?"

A More Lasting Identity

The trouble with attaching one's identity to something that passes becomes clear when the thing is gone. To paraphrase

Erich Fromm: "If I am what I do and what I do is lost, who then am I?"

. . .

When I quit swimming in college I had no idea who I was. All my life I'd been "Dick Roth, swimmer." It was not uncommon for someone to say, "I want you to meet Dick Roth. He's a swimmer." Or I'd overhear something like, "There goes Dick Roth— you know, the swimmer."

I thought they were right. I got my fulfillment from what I did in the pool. I felt good when I swam well and bad when I didn't. If I won a big race or set a record, I'd feel good for months. When I got beaten after being on top for a while, I was devastated.

When my swimming career ended, I went through a classic identity crisis. It was ugly. I was directionless, without purpose, and almost lifeless. I no longer knew who I was.

I had become what I did, and what I did was gone.

. . .

Even before midlife, we ought to be repeatedly asking ourselves questions like these:

"What won't pass away when my youth does?"

"Who will I be after my career is over?"

"Who would I be if everything else was gone but my mind and feelings?"

I picked up an extraordinary little book, *The Diving Bell and the Butterfly*, by Jean-Dominique Bauby. The author had been completely paralyzed by a stroke, except for one eyelid. He wrote the entire book by communicating the only way he could: slowly forming words and sentences by blinking his eye as a transcriber called out the letters of the alphabet.

Amazing as the whole thing was, the story of his confinement within the "diving bell" of his body was most impressive to me because of Bauby's total lack of self-pity. He still was able to see his soul as a butterfly. I highly recommend this moving book to anyone enduring a midlife crisis, or anyone feeling sorry for himself or herself. Reading just a few pages should help you to treasure the life you have.

As I read Bauby's book, I wondered what I'd be like if all I had under my control were an eyelid. What would I have left to give? Could I ever be happy? Content? Peaceful? What if I couldn't even blink my eye? What if all I had left was my consciousness? Who would I be then?

Before finding out about Frankl and Selye, like most of us I looked for answers in the wrong places. Recently I was given this quote from writer Shakti Gawain which, to me, says perfectly where to find the answers:

"Often people attempt to live their lives backwards. They try to have more things, or more money, in order to do more of what they want, so that they will be happier. The way it actually works is the reverse. You must first be who you really are, then do what you need to do, in order to have what you want."

We first need to find out who we would be if everything were stripped away. Only then should we be concerned with what we do. Or, as the current wisdom goes, we need to be "human beings" before we turn into "human doings."

So who would you be if all the things you have and do were taken away?

To come up with an answer, try saying something like: "I am . . ." and fill in the blank. But don't fill it in with something like, "I am a manager" or "I am a salesman." You might find more durable answers in words that express inner qualities, such as honesty, courage, compassion, and so forth.

A better way to phrase the statement might be this: "I am a man of . . . ."

When you have finished doing what you do in life, you still can be honest, or grateful, or compassionate. No matter what you have or don't have, you can always be a man of integrity, or sincerity, or whatever. What's most important is that you fill in the blank for yourself.

Then nobody can ever take it away from you. And when you begin to align your actions with your ideals, so that what you do expresses who you are, you aren't living life "backwards" anymore.

The source of your security then becomes internal and lasting. When you get your meaning from your intrinsic nature, your life will have a meaning that can never end.

• • •

Only after you have gained a strong inner sense of self is it possible to approach your relationships with the power of humility. In the next chapter, we'll look at ways to apply that intrinsic strength in order to help your evolving marriage grow and deepen.

12. Your Relationship

I've been giving you a lot of advice about how to relate to your wife. It probably sounds like all I'm saying is "Be understanding," "Listen to her," and "Be supportive." But what about when you don't feel like it? What if, in the face of her moods and needs, you really want to yell, fight back, or run away?

Good questions, for which there are no easy answers.

• • •

During my wife's menopause, quite a bit of the time the issues that came up were clearly more about her emotions and physical changes than mine. That was when it was good for me to do a lot of listening.

But there were also times when I should have spoken more. Unfortunately, I am not particularly good at expressing myself when it's difficult or emotional.

Like a lot of men (and a lot of women, too), most of my life I've bottled up what I've felt if I considered it negative. Instead of being honest, I usually put on some kind of "Mr. Nice" exterior.

Besides being inauthentic, the trouble with this strategy is that it only works in the short term.

Man, I wish I'd done better here. In the name of maintaining harmony, I left some things unsaid that I really wanted to talk about. But ignoring important issues doesn't make them go away. Usually, for a little while, I was able to exhibit behavior that looked caring and considerate. But when it was a put-on, it didn't work for long.

As a result, I had some memorable eruptions. After a slow simmer, I'd find myself suddenly boiling just under the surface. What in reality was a small issue had been growing into a big one in my mind.

Life has a way of breaking down our contrivances and forcing us to be honest. Maybe I'd be tired, or worried about something else. Maybe my emotional buttons would get pushed in some unrelated but sensitive area.

Anyway, whatever the trigger, I'd go Vesuvian. All of my bottled up feelings would come out, ugly and all at once. Without warning, I'd be yelling, screaming, hitting walls, and throwing things. It was not a pretty picture. I ended up hoarse more than once. And I had to repair a wall or two.

I also had to repair my marriage.

Three Foundational Ideas

Before I offer any suggestions about how to communicate effectively so as to avoid exploding the way I used to do (and sometimes still do), let me suggest three foundational ideas that underlie all the specifics I'll propose:

1. To be successful, both sides of any relationship must benefit. Over the long term there can't be winners and losers. Both halves of a marriage need to feel good about how it's going.
2. The techniques offered as part of the solutions will work only if your heart is in the right place and if your actions reflect your heart's motives.

3. Remember to stop and smell the roses every so often. Fun should be a part of every stage of life, especially midlife.

1. Relationships Are Two-Sided

I don't believe that the burden of making a marriage work during a woman's menopause rests solely with her male partner. But I have tried to convey the impression that, when a woman is going through the stresses of menopause, a man needs to do a lot, if not most, of what it takes to keep the marriage functioning smoothly. It may mean learning some new skills, such as listening, being patient and understanding, and not trying to fix our wives' problems. These skills are crucial, but by themselves they are insufficient, because relationships are always two-sided.

During the menopausal passage, it is often wise to put your wife's needs ahead of yours. But I take some good counsel here from Stephen Covey, among others. In his book, *The Seven Habits of Highly Effective People*, Covey suggests that for any long-term relationship to be successful, both parties should *always seek mutual benefit*. There are two sets of needs to be fulfilled. Mutual benefit means: don't forget her needs, *and* don't forget your own needs either.

If you haven't read Stephen Covey's books, I suggest starting with *The Seven Habits*, paying special attention to Habits Four, Five, and Six, which he calls "the habits of interdependence." If you have already read this valuable book, I recommend that you reread at least these three chapters.

2. Check Your Motives

While it's important for you to take care of both your wife's needs and your own, it's *critical* to remember that you're not taking care of your wife so that you can get *your* needs met. When you listen, listen just because you want to, never because you want anything in return. Speak your feelings because you need to, not because you think that if you do you'll fulfill some obligation.

You must first be aware of your motives; then let your behavior authentically demonstrate them. Your actions should express what you feel, not cover over or belie your feelings. If you don't want to say what you feel, don't. If you don't want to understand, don't act as if you want to. As you listen, your wife should be able to feel the honesty of your intent to understand, and not sense some phony or partial listening, or some listening that makes you look politically correct.

Don't expect anything back. I won't be offering any quick-fix techniques that you can "do to" your wife to get something in return. It's not a formula. Your giving must be unconditional.

But ironically, when you give unconditionally, that's when you get the most in return.

3. Smell the Roses

Reading about midlife and menopause can make you feel like you're going to have to walk through some kind of painful purgatory between adulthood and geezerhood. So I want to assure you that, even though the journey can be tough at times, there's lots of room for fun along the way.

We need to lighten up occasionally, to take time to notice how good things are. Getting this far along in your life is a whole lot better than the alternative.

Make some menopause jokes—like the title for this book. My wife and I still use it to get a giggle. Laugh about your midlife crisis. I must be in a long one, because my family has been calling my last two cars "midlife crisis cars."

There's a great book out called *Menopaws*, a collection of cartoons about menopawsal cats. Buy it. Read it. Share it with your wife. I bet you'll both laugh out loud. Leave it lying around the house. Our copy is on the coffee table in the living room. My favorite cartoon is on page 31. Look it up.

If all we did at midlife was sit around and introspect about our identities, identify our feelings, and talk about menopause, life could get pretty seriously dull. We need to give all the seriousness a rest every now and then. Life is to be experienced *right now*. Every soul needs to have some fun.

Do something spontaneous, out of the ordinary, or even outrageous. Get off the couch or out of your chair. Suggest to your mate that the two of you go to an opera, a play, or maybe the zoo. Get in the car and drive somewhere without knowing where you're going. Go out dancing with some kids thirty years younger than you. Find a Mongolian restaurant, go bowling, buy flowers, read poetry out loud to each other, whatever; just remember to have some fun.

As I move into some specific suggestions about how we can keep our relationships strong and growing throughout midlife, remember the ground rules: seek mutual benefit; keep your motives pure and unconditional; and, please, remember to smell the roses.

Understanding and Education Come First

Once again, there is nothing our wives want more from us during menopause than for us to understand what they're going through.

The first step to this understanding is getting a general education. That is, learn the menopause basics. I hope that, by this point in the book, we've accomplished that goal.

But book learning can only take you so far, so please don't think that reading this book is enough. The next step is to talk to your wife about her menopause. Find out what's going on from her perspective; understand her specific changes. How is her menopause unique? Does she see menopause as a positive transition? Is she dreading it or looking forward to it? Is she bothered, or sailing right through it? What emotions does she feel? Does she get anxious, worried, or grouchy? How aware of her moods is she? Is she getting enough sleep? Does sex hurt her? What does she feel about getting acupuncture? Taking hormones? Taking herbs? Is she getting enough calcium? Vitamin D? Exercise? What kind of doctor does she want? Does she want help from you? What kind?

This is a long list, but only a partial one. It's just a starting point, a way to open up a dialogue. Believe me, the benefits of getting the dialogue going will be more than worth the effort. Understanding what is going on with your wife will make a world of difference to you. You won't be mystified. You can inwardly say to yourself, "Oh, I get it. That's why she seems worried." Or, "So that's why she doesn't want sex." Or, "Oh. I had no idea she felt that way."

But the process of gaining understanding is easier said than done. Males as a gender, and perhaps Americans as a society, tend to be better at understanding information than feelings. Much of the time, such as at work or in school, this tendency toward logic has served us well. But, in trying to understand your wife's experience of menopause, getting to know how she feels can be even more important than understanding how she thinks.

A word of caution: Try to understand your spouse's feelings without judging them as good or bad. When we judge another as wrong—even silently—we tend to make that person defensive. It's much more important to help someone discover why they feel the way they feel than to tell them that the way they feel is wrong.

I know that I'm being idealistic here. When my wife is angry at the world, it's easy for me to be dispassionate, nonjudgmental, and supportive. But when she's angry at me, it's a whole different story. I rarely stay nice, logical, and detached. Regardless, trying to understand feelings without judging them is a worthy effort.

The easiest way I know to find out how someone is feeling is simply to ask. Something like "How are you feeling?" works well. Or maybe try "What do you feel about . . ." and fill in the blank with something like ". . . your doctor?" or ". . . taking hormones?"

or "... sex these days?" I know these questions sound simple, but try them. You can open up a wonderfully illuminating conversation.

One of the benefits to listening with the genuine intent to understand is that you learn. Don't assume that you know what your wife feels. Be prepared to learn something new. You might find it fun or meaningful, maybe even impressive or challenging.

If, by contrast, you listen and judge your wife's feelings, and you respond with a certain revealing expression on your face, or with words like, "You shouldn't feel that way," you could shut her up and cut off future opportunities to communicate, understand, and learn.

Another important and commonsense point is to try listening first, before expressing yourself. This good advice was first put forward by the noted American psychologist Carl Rogers. It is not *easy* advice, but it's good. There are two key elements of this simple idea. First is the sequence: listen first, talk second. The second key is to remember that communication is always two-sided. Yes, listen first to what she feels, and then don't forget to express your own feelings in turn.

This second key about expressing your feelings presupposes that you know what you feel.

Knowing Your Feelings

On the most fundamental level, feelings can usually be described with one word: happy, sad, angry, cheerful, hurt, afraid, elated, frustrated, tired, joyful, overwhelmed, exhilarated, discombobulated, and so forth. There are lots of feelings, and lots of words to describe them. But coming up with a list is the easy part.

The hard part is awareness—being aware right now of how you feel. Try saying to yourself, "I'm ..." and filling in the blank with a feeling word. Sounds easy, and maybe right now it is easy. But feelings can be complex. You might feel angry right now, for instance, but it could be because you're afraid, and maybe you were taught that men shouldn't be afraid, and you're actually embarrassed. So rather than show your fear, you show anger instead. You're not really angry; that's just on the surface. Look a little deeper and you find that you're afraid.

Another difficulty in recognizing your feelings is learning not to place the responsibility for a feeling with anyone else. Instead of saying, "You make me feel . . . ," just say "I feel . . ." Or instead of thinking something like, "She's being bitchy," try saying to yourself, "I'm upset" or "I'm mad" or "I'm frustrated," or whatever it is that you feel.

If identifying your feelings sounds simplistic and easy to you as you sit reading, just wait. In the ups and downs of a relationship, becoming aware of emotions can be extremely difficult. Especially if your feelings happen to be intense, or if you think somebody else is causing them, or if you're in the middle of an argument.

Don't worry if you're not very good at spotting how you feel when you first start trying; I don't think anybody is. Keep trying, because clearly identifying your feelings and acknowledging them as your own become important when it's time to say what they are.

Communicating Your Feelings

Communicating how you feel may be hard because it's something pretty new for you, or maybe you don't know how, or maybe you find it hard to talk about yourself.

But once you've listened and you've done your best to become aware of how you feel, there's still one more key rule: express yourself. Don't "stuff your feelings." Don't hold them inside. Remember, communication is two-sided. When it's your turn to talk, don't chicken out.

For some of us, the problem may not be that we don't take our turn, but that we don't do it effectively. That is, we may talk, but we don't get heard.

Five Ground Rules for Communicating

I want to recommend the following ground rules for communicating when it's your turn.

1. Be Both Courageous and Considerate

Another piece of wisdom from Stephen Covey that has helped me tremendously, both generally and in particular during my wife's menopause, is to try to approach a relationship—any relationship—with *a balance of courage and consideration.* This means having the courage to say what's on your mind while being considerate as you say it.

Being considerate can mean more than thinking about the other person's needs, or giving the other a chance to speak. It can mean checking out your attitude. Are you saying the right words, but with a sneer or a tone of voice that makes them mean something else? Are you listening, but doing it with that smug look on your face that says "Yeah, but . . ."?

Some people have no trouble being courageous enough to say what they feel. They just blurt the words right out without thinking. I used to do that, but I found that usually people didn't hear me, or they reacted to me by getting defensive. I was plenty courageous, saying exactly what I needed to say. But my attitude wasn't making my relationships any better, because I only considered *my* feelings, not the other person's.

I learned. Now, as I said, I tend to try to create harmony by being understanding and nice. But when I go too far over to the consideration side, I end up bottling up my feelings until they fester. I unconsciously stew. At one time, menopause gave me an excuse to think this was OK. I was justifying my lack of courage in the name of being supportive. But, as somebody once said, "Unexpressed feelings never die, they just get buried alive and come out later in uglier ways."

Effective relationships require a *balance* of courage and consideration. If you're like me, you'll learn through trial and error, through swinging from one extreme to the other until you achieve that balance. But whatever you do, don't give up. This one is really worth it.

2. Develop an Awareness of Timing

Perhaps the best time to talk about a feeling is when you feel it least intensely. A psychologist friend of mine tells me that the average feeling, if left to run its course, will arise and subside within three minutes. If what you're feeling could be explosive, it might take a little longer, but just a little patience can do a lot to defuse the situation. Let your feelings subside, let hers subside, and then have a discussion.

Don't duck the issue, just be sensitive about your timing. You still need to be honest, you still need to get your feelings out in the open, and you still need to say everything that you need to say.

Think about when, in the course of your day or even your week, you could bring up the issue rationally and considerately. This may mean choosing a time when neither you nor your wife is tired, hungry, or upset. I've found myself much more able to speak my feelings respectfully in the mornings, when I'm not tired. And I try to choose a time when neither one of us is upset. I need to concentrate all my energy and strength on being considerate, if I want to do it well. So I also like to choose a time and place that I'm not likely to be distracted.

Those few times when I've managed to handle my need to be heard in a mature way, I've waited until I've cooled down, and then I've said something like this: "Susan, I need to say some things. I feel like I'm gonna explode if I don't get it out."

For us, this has worked. I've gotten to say what I wanted to, and my wife has gotten to hear it.

Some couples have found that setting aside a regular time of the week, say an hour each Sunday morning, makes it easier for them to talk. That way, no one has to ask for time. Other couples, when going through difficult times, save their discussions for restaurants or other public places, where they find themselves much more likely to remain respectful and civil.

3. Remember: There's Nothing to Fix

One of my biggest fears about writing this book has been that I'll give you too much information. I'm afraid I'll contribute to a situation where you approach your wife as if you know what's the matter with her, and can tell her what to do to make it all better.

Remember that there's nothing wrong with her. She's just going through menopause, so there's nothing to fix. You are not a mechanic; you're her husband.

First of all, acting like there's something wrong can contribute to her feeling "broken," something she definitely doesn't need to feel. Secondly, this attitude can be condescending, which is probably the least productive way to approach your relationship. You are neither Mr. Fix-It nor Mr. Know-It-All.

4. Say It Without Pushing Her Buttons

If you've been with your partner for more that just a few years, you probably are an unconscious expert at knowing what to say and just the right way to say it to really upset her. We rarely employ this devilish little skill consciously, but watch yourself in your next argument. I'll bet you push her emotional buttons more than once, and I'll bet you're really good at it.

Irritating your wife is often a knee-jerk reaction to getting your own buttons pushed, and results in a rapidly escalating argument. As my wife says, "When we get hurt, we want to hurt back." You need to develop a high degree of awareness to notice that what you are saying is unconsciously designed to bother her. Usually, you'll see the effects of your words only after the fact. Even when you're aware enough to notice your tendencies, you will have to apply liberal amounts of willpower to keep yourself from unconsciously intensifying an argument.

But, once again, the benefits of a good discussion are worth the effort.

5. Speak Inoffensively About Yourself

Earlier, when I was talking about knowing your feelings, I advised you to try not to connect the way you feel with someone else's actions. In other words, think something like "I feel sad" instead of "She makes me sad." When it's your turn to speak, this same rule applies: speak about your own feelings, not about the other person's actions. Your wife can probably keep her defenses a lot lower if you say "I'm feeling down" or "I'm upset," rather than "You really make me mad." This might be the only time when it's entirely appropriate to be self-centered and talk only about you.

If you're like many men, you'll experience a tendency to blame your feelings on your wife's menopause. You might want to say: "You're really upsetting me because you're so bitchy these days." Or maybe: "I'm always walking on eggshells around you because I never know what kind of mood you're going to be in." Talk about pushing buttons . . . these are not productive ways to begin a discussion.

More productive and, with a little deeper look, much more honest, would be to say something solely about yourself, such as: "I'm confused. I don't know what you need from me."

You can also describe your feelings in ways that will raise fewer defensive reactions. Hearing that you're "upset" will probably go down a lot better than hearing that you're "really pissed off." Saying that you feel "annoyed" will probably be heard better than "I'm sick and tired . . ."

Further, if you can assign yourself a vulnerable, non-macho feeling, which is often the most authentic take on the situation anyway, you should be heard even better. Instead of "I'm mad . . . ," see if you can work with the complexity of the feeling until you find the deeper layers. Then you might end up saying instead something like "I'm embarrassed . . ." which will be much more honest. And it's sure to be much more appreciated.

To put it all together, try to speak about *yourself* in an inoffensive and vulnerable way, rather than talking aggressively about what *she* does.

• • •

"This advice you're giving me is all well and good," you may be saying, "but what if I try it and it doesn't work? What if I'm just not that good at it?" Or you may be thinking, "This all sounds good on paper, but what if I'm so mad that there's no way I can be Mr. Nice?"

Those are good questions, and real ones. Relationships are not easy. I wish I were good at them. Sometimes I just can't find the consideration, or the vulnerability, or the right words.

But remember: "Unexpressed feelings never die . . . "

Discharging Your Feelings Elsewhere

If your feelings remain explosive, you'd better find somewhere else to discharge the energy. And I don't mean into an affair. You could go out to the woods and yell really loud, go to the gym and sweat, run till your lungs burn, talk to somebody who'll listen, get some help from a therapist, or whatever.

There are ways to let off steam that you won't later regret. Try to find a place where you can safely express your anger, or your need to be right, or your need to win.

• • •

I was lucky in this respect. Toward the end of my wife's menopause, I took a trip down the Colorado River in the Grand Canyon with a dozen men about my age. Our trip wasn't planned as therapy, but it ended up having that effect.

It was the first time in years that any of us had been alone for any period of time with just men. That was where the unexpected therapy lay.

After a couple of days of being careful about what we said—that is, being politically correct—we started to revert to being men (boys?). We burped, farted, swore, talked about sex, competed with each other, told dirty jokes, and got downright stinky.

We were just a bunch of men being men together.

It was a great release. Just to let that male part of me be male was exhilarating. I didn't have to apologize for it. I didn't have to control it. Damn but it was fun!

It's not that I want to be that way all the time, but not letting that competitive male part of me live and breathe had been pretty stifling.

By letting it come out on the river trip, I gave voice to a part of me that might soon have reared up and hurt my relationship. In the name of wanting to be nice, I had been trying hard not to be competitive with my wife. I'd even been trying not to try to win any arguments. For years I'd been quieting my macho side, trying not to look too smart, or be too aggressive, or be the center of attention.

On the river, it sure was fun to let go and just be me.

Denying who we are is pretty unhealthy. Yet parts of us can be pretty destructive if they erupt at the wrong time. The key, I think, is to find a time and a place where we can be who we are without it being harmful to others. We all need a release once in a while.

Partners in the Process

Some menopause authorities are advising women to become partners with us in the process we are going through.

I like the paradigm shift here. So far, I've mostly been talking about men being partners with their wives in the menopause process. But we certainly are going through our own transitions—maybe unwillingly, but we're changing just the same.

All the advice I've given you about how to relate to your wife can work in reverse. In this area, turnabout definitely is fair play. But if your partner isn't accustomed to being approached when you need a listening ear, you might have to take the initiative and ask for her time, energy, and support.

Most of us need somebody to talk to from time to time. Who better than your wife? Try asking her to listen to how you feel about what's happening deep inside you. See if it doesn't do you some good. Beware: it may feel so good that you'll want her to listen to you again and again. Being deeply listened to might even be so therapeutic that you'll want to return the favor to your wife.

Watch out, though. If you do enough of this, you may end up in a really excellent relationship.

Another way to honor your growth process and deepen your partnership is to tell your mate what you need. I hope that by now you know what she needs. While it may be unusual for a man to talk about it, it's not rare for a man to want a little time alone for reflection. Maybe you just want an hour occasionally. Or maybe you'd like to head out alone for a few days of camping. Or you might want to rent a beach house by yourself for a week. Some men like to go on retreats, or go to men's groups, or they like to float down the Colorado with a group of guys.

Maybe, in addition to needing some time alone, you want to change jobs, or reconnect with your family, or spend more time with your kids. Or it could be that you want to write, or take a painting class, or get back into playing your guitar. Or maybe you just want to hang out and do nothing.

Tell her about it.

• • •

"Okay," you may be saying, "that all sounds like a pretty good idea. But what if she won't listen?"

That's a possibility. And that's exactly why I've written the next chapter. Ask her to read it.

13 A Word to the Wives

Most middle-aged husbands (according to a Gallup poll, about two-thirds of us) are pretty concerned about our wives' menopause. On this subject, that's a whole lot more worried men than worried women. You women are beginning to challenge the myths of menopause and to come to some understanding of it, but we men, it appears, are still largely in the dark.

Worried Men

We husbands worry about menopause for a lot of surface reasons. Some of us fear that you are going to become terminally cranky. Some of us worry that our sex lives will go south. Some of us are afraid that our beautiful wife will grow a hump in her back, or get wrinkly, or let herself go.

But, beneath the surface, there may be deeper fears. We may not want to admit it, but deep down many of us would like to deny the countless little ways that we're getting older. We may have noticed our graying hair, or that it's a whole lot harder to keep the weight off, try as we might. The young women don't look at us any more. And even if we haven't admitted it to you, a lot of us don't need sex quite as often, or can't perform as well as we used to. (Hence the enormous success of Viagra.)

149

The book entitled *Male Menopause* may have raised some masculine eyebrows, or caused some of us to chuckle in disbelief. But a lot of us men wondered if it could possibly be true: could that be what's going on? Could we be going through some kind of menopause, too?

Our wives' menopause may be raising our awareness that we are past the halfway point in our lives. As a result, a lot of husbands may be going through some pretty serious questioning, a midlife crisis maybe. Some of us wonder if what we have been chasing is all there is to life. Many of us have climbed the corporate ladder. Some have the house, the cars, the super-fast laptop.

But we may have noticed that all the success hasn't made us as happy as we thought it would. Or maybe we feel that we haven't achieved as much as we envisioned. Perhaps the reality of our life falls short of our expectations.

So some of us men, at this time of our lives, are looking for something more, but we have no clue as to what it is. Many of us may change our jobs at midlife. Others just want an opportunity to take a break, or want to have some time to reflect and to figure out what's going on inside ourselves.

Clueless Men

Many of us husbands may not have given our wives' menopause a whole lot of conscious preliminary thought. If they're like me, they haven't wanted to believe that menopause and aging would ever happen. But the first time our wives opened a window on a chilly night or yelled at us when we had no idea why, many of our worst subconscious fears might have come suddenly to life. A partner who is going through menopause can seem so unpredictable and moody to an unprepared husband.

Many husbands really have no idea what's going on, but we certainly would like to. We might know that the moods and the hot flashes mean our wives are in menopause, but we may not be exactly sure what that means. Some of us may have read an article or two on it, because we keep finding open magazines strategically placed around the house. Some may have even looked through a menopause book that appeared on the bed-side table. But this doesn't mean that *your* husband knows what's happening with *you*. He may know some generalizations, but he needs you to share your own specifics.

You could be thinking, as you read this, that a lot of men are pretty bad listeners. True enough. But a caring husband, regard-less of his skills, really does want to know what's up about your menopause. Give your man a try; tell him what your concerns are; let him know what you're doing about them.

A lot of us husbands would be more than willing to help if we knew what it was our partners wanted. More help around the house? A back rub? Some time with us? Some time alone? Some of us may be a little unaccustomed to asking, so you may have to seize the initiative. Believe it or not, though, most men are decent humans who want to know how to help.

Some Unsolicited Advice

In response to what men tell me they consider important, may I offer you five specific pieces of advice?

First, try to tell your husband what kind of mood you're in before he makes a stupid mistake and sticks his foot in his mouth. Are you tired? On edge? Would you like some help? He will be much more likely to respond appropriately if you can tell him how you feel.

Second, try to tell your husband how you feel with as much consideration for his feelings as possible. He's only human. He reacts to attitudes just as much as anyone else.

Third, you should talk to him about what's happening with you and sex. Some husbands are pretty worried. Reassure him that your changing feelings have to do with menopause, not with him. Explain to him what's going on for you. Are there simple things that would make sex more comfortable for you? Would you prefer more communication? More cuddling? More foreplay?

Fourth, try a little humor. Everybody needs a good laugh every now and then.

Fifth, even men need partners and friends. Looking at the last half of life can be frightening. Everyone can use someone to talk it over with. True, you might need to encourage your husband to talk; he may not know how to begin. Or he may be embarrassed. Many men aren't comfortable admitting that they're afraid they've made some mistakes. Some even wonder if their whole lives may have been going in the wrong direction—not an easy thing for anyone to admit. Ask him about what he's going through. Ask him how he feels. He needs a good listener, too.

If your husband is like me, once he gets going he enjoys talking about himself. Just get us started and we're likely to give you an earful—more than you might want.

You might have to develop a new skill: shutting us up.

We men realize that the intensity of your menopause has the potential to deepen our relationship with you. A lot of us might even be ready for that.

A Positive Perspective
From a Female Physician

In closing, I want to tell you about one doctor, Susan Love, who has come up with a fascinating paradigm shift. In her meticulously researched book, *Dr. Susan Love's Hormone Book: Making Informed Choices About Menopause*, co-authored by Karen Lindsey, she takes a completely fresh approach to the whole issue of menopause.

She starts by noting that women like Eleanor Roosevelt, Golda Meir, and Margaret Thatcher became world leaders *after* menopause. They are great examples of what Margaret Mead called "postmenopausal zest." Their accomplishments demonstrated that they couldn't possibly have been suffering from a "deficiency disease."

Dr. Love posits that maybe it's not that women have too little estrogen after menopause; perhaps they had too much of it before. She suggests, only half jokingly, that premenopausal women might have been suffering from "estrogen poisoning."

She goes on to note that, biologically, the human race probably needs women to have forty years of that much estrogen, in order to ensure the continuance of the race. "But maybe," she says, "when our biological responsibility is taken care of, we're allowed to be freed of those domesticating hormones and can reclaim our eight-year-old self again, full of beans and ready to take on the world."

I wish you much happiness in your personal process of self-reclamation.

Resources

I don't want to overwhelm you with these pages of resources, but I do want to point you in the direction of further help and information. Some of the following material may be a lot more useful to your wife than to you, and actually it's for her that I'm including it. Remember: if you take a pushy or know-it-all stance, relaying this menopause information to her could actually be counterproductive. So be sensitive.

Books

Menopause in General

Dr. Susan Love's Hormone Book: Making Informed Choices About Menopause
Susan Love, M.D., with Karen Lindsey
This is unquestionably at the top of my list of menopause books. Love and Lindsey have created the most comprehensive and readable encyclopedia of menopause available. In my opinion, if your wife has only one menopause book in her collection, this should be the one.

The Silent Passage: Menopause
Gail Sheehy
This is the first popular menopause book and still one of the best— valuable even a decade after its release. By making her personal journey available to women through her writing, Sheehy has set an example that's changing the way menopause is viewed throughout America and the world. Excellent.

155

Turning Point: The Myths and Realities of Menopause
C. Sue Furman
This is the best book I found for technical detail about the biology of menopause. If you liked Chapter Two in this book, about how a woman's body works, you'll love Furman's book.

Women of the 14th Moon: Writings on Menopause
Edited by Dena Taylor and Amber Coverdale Sumrall
I highly recommend this book to any man (or woman) who wants to know what menopause actually feels like. The short essays cover menopause from every conceivable angle. The poetry is enlightening. If you're like me, the essay by Mary Lou Logothetis on pages 40 to 45 will turn your head around.

Proponents of HRT

Feminine Forever
Robert A. Wilson, M.D.
This is the classic that started it all. If you can find it, it's well worth the reading. Try looking in your library. I found my copy through The Book Web, a seller of used books on the Internet at www.thebookweb.com.

Managing Your Menopause
Wulf H. Utian, M.D., Ph.D., and Ruth S. Jacobowitz
Dr. Utian is a highly respected and dedicated menopause authority who has helped countless women with his menopause program. He also began the North American Menopause Society (see Web Sites, below). Utian and Jacobowitz outline the risks and benefits of HRT and counsel women to make their own decision, then outline a complete program that includes HRT as one component.

Estrogen: A Complete Guide to Reversing the Effects of Menopause Using Hormone Replacement Therapy
Lila Nachtigall, M.D., and Joan Rattner Heilman
Dr. Nachtigall is an unabashed proponent of HRT. This book, like others she has written, makes strong arguments for the benefits of estrogen supplements.

Alternatives to HRT

What Your Doctor May Not Tell You About Menopause:
The Breakthrough Book on Natural Progesterone
John R. Lee, M.D., with Virginia Hopkins
Dr. Lee is the natural-progesterone pioneer. His book has been a welcome relief to thousands of women who wished for some menopausal remedy beyond synthetic hormones. His wisdom provided the first breakthrough for my wife, who has recommended it to many of her friends. My wife and I, along with countless women, remain grateful to Dr. Lee.

Natural Hormone Replacement for Women Over 45
Jonathan V. Wright, M.D., and John Morgenthaler
This is another breakthrough book. Dr. Wright is one of the early and also foremost practitioners of a full hormonal alternative to HRT, which he calls NHR (natural hormone replacement). The book is quick and easy to read, but is quite thorough. It will be very helpful to any woman who wants to try hormones but is unsure about using synthetics.

Natural Woman, Natural Menopause
Marcus Laux, N.D., and Christine Conrad
Dr. Laux is a leading naturopathic menopause practitioner, as well as a professor at the National College of Naturopathic Medicine. His perspective on menopause has been a valuable addition to the literature on this subject. Christine Conrad founded the Natural Woman Institute. Their book details a complete natural program for menopausal women that includes natural hormones, diet, and exercise.

Menopause as a Transition

Menopausal Years: The Wise Woman Way
Susun S. Weed
This is the book that gave me the impetus to write my own book. The idea that menopause could be a valuable stage of life was such an "Aha!" to me that I wanted to share it with other husbands. Susun Weed is an herbalist—perhaps the foremost expert on menopausal herbs—so her book is also recommended for women who prefer herbs to hormones.

Red Moon Passage: The Power and Wisdom of Menopause
Bonnie J. Horrigan
This book is a collection of personal stories of women who look at menopause as a time of transformation and regeneration. Horrigan is a leader in the movement of women who view menopause as an archetypal or spiritual journey.

Hysterectomy

The Hysterectomy Hoax
Stanley West, M.D., with Paula Dranov
As you can tell from the title, this book does not look favorably at hysterectomies. I was spellbound, but shocked, by this powerful book. I recommend it for women who are considering a hysterectomy (and for their husbands), but not for women who have had the surgery.

For Men

Male Menopause
Jed Diamond
If you are a man in your forties or fifties, you really should read this book. Diamond has done us all a favor with his thorough research. He explains what we are all experiencing, both physically and psychologically, as we age. Just becoming aware that there is such a thing as "male menopause" (or, if you prefer to be technically correct, viropause or andropause) is worth the price of the book. Understanding what this passage actually does to men can be tremendously reassuring.

Understanding Men's Passages: Discovering the
New Map of Men's Lives
Gail Sheehy
Gail Sheehy has done it again. This book really got to me. It felt like Sheehy had been inside my head, watching my thoughts. If I had had the chance to read it before I wrote my book, there would have been many a reference to her wisdom. It helps me know that there are many of you guys out there with challenges and experiences like mine. I firmly believe that every man at midlife could benefit from this book.

Associations

American College for Advancement in Medicine, (800) 532-3688

American Osteopathic Association, (312) 202-8000

American Association of Naturopathic Physicians, (206) 298-0125

National Commission for the Certification of Acupuncturists, (703) 548-9004

American College of Obstetrics and Gynecology, (202) 638-5577, Ext. 2518

For Referrals to Compounding Pharmacists

The International Academy of Compounding Pharmacists (IACP), (800) 927-4227

Professional Compounding Centers of America (PCCA), (800) 331-2498

Women's Support Organizations

The National Women's Health Network
(202) 628-7814
This is a Washington, D.C.-based women's advocacy/lobbying group, specializing in women's health issues. The telephone number is for their information clearinghouse, a great source of menopause information.

Women's Health America
(608) 833-9102
This is the information number for the Madison Pharmacy, one of the country's preeminent compounding pharmacies specializing in women's health. You can get information here regarding how compounding pharmacists can help with menopause.

Newsletters

A Friend Indeed
   (514) 843-5730

Hot Flash: Newsletter for Midlife and Older Women
   (212) 725-8625

Menopause News
   (800) 241-6366

Web Sites

A couple of cautions about the Internet:
   Web sites come and Web sites go. I have tried to choose a few that look like they might be around for a while. A good way to tell how current they are is to look them up using a search engine to see when they were last modified. (I don't know if all search engines show that information, but AltaVista and Infoseek do.)
   The Internet, including these Web sites, can cause information overload, so be careful how you present this to your wife. She could be on overload already.

Women's Health – Menopause
www.ama-assn.org/insight/h_focus/wom_hlth/menopaus
Sponsored by the AMA, this is a good site for learning the basics of menopause.

North American Menopause Society
www.menopause.org
The North American Menopause Society is a professional organization for doctors and other health care practitioners. The group's Web site is an excellent source of information and includes pages of good links.

Menopause Online
www.menopause-online.com
An interesting site with current news releases about menopause drugs and treatments.

Dynamic Living/About Women
www.aboutwomen.com/menopause/wwwboard
A bulletin board that looks very helpful.
Atlanta Reproductive Health Center – Menopause
www.ivf.com/meno
This site is informative and chock-full of menopause links.

Power Surge
www.dearest.com
This is a menopause-support network on the Internet. This site rocks.
Check it out. It has everything you ever wanted to know about
menopause—with music, too. Unlike a lot of Web sites, this one feels
friendly.

$\mathcal{B}$ibliography

Apter, Terri. *Secret Paths: Women in the New Midlife*. New York: W. W. Norton, 1995.

Barbach, Lonnie, Ph.D. *The Pause: Positive Approaches to Menopause*. New York: Penguin Books, 1993.

Bauby, Jean-Dominique. *The Diving Bell and the Butterfly*. New York: Alfred A. Knopf, 1997.

Borysenko, Joan, Ph.D. *A Woman's Book of Life: The Biology, Psychology, and Spirituality of the Feminine Life Cycle*. New York: Riverhead Books, 1996.

Brehony, Kathleen A. *Awakening at Midlife: A Guide to Reviving Your Spirit, Recreating Your Life, and Returning to Your Truest Self*. New York: Riverhead Books, 1996.

Cone, Faye Kitchener. *Making Sense of Menopause*. New York: Simon and Schuster, 1993.

Coney, Sandra. *The Menopause Industry: How the Medical Establishment Exploits Women*. Alameda, Calif.: Hunter House, 1994.

Covey, Stephen R. *The Seven Habits of Highly Effective People*. New York: Simon and Schuster, 1989.

Covey, Stephen R., A. Roger Merrill and Rebecca R. Merrill. *First Things First*. New York: Simon and Schuster, 1994.

Cutler, Winnifred B., Ph.D., and Celso-Ramon Garcia, M.D. *Menopause: A Guide for Women and Those Who Love Them*. New York: W.W. Norton, 1983.

Diamond, Jed. *Male Menopause*. Naperville, Ill.: Sourcebooks, 1997.

Dickson, Anne and Nikki Henriques. *Women on Menopause: A Practical Guide to a Positive Transition*. Rochester, Vt.: Healing Arts Press, 1988.

Dosh, Robert M., Ph.D., et al. *The Taking Charge of Menopause Workbook*. Oakland, Calif.: New Harbinger Publications, 1997.

163

Fisher, Roger, and William Ury. *Getting to Yes: Negotiating Agreement Without Giving In.* New York: Viking Penguin, 1981.

Frankl, Viktor E. *Man's Search for Meaning: An Introduction to Logotherapy.* New York: Simon and Schuster, 1959.

Friedan, Betty. *The Fountain of Age.* New York: Simon and Schuster, 1993.

Furman, C. Sue. *Turning Point: The Myths and Realities of Menopause.* New York: Oxford University Press, 1995.

Gray, John, Ph.D., *Men Are From Mars, Women Are From Venus: A Practical Guide for Improving Communication and Getting What You Want in Your Relationships.* New York: HarperCollins, 1992.

Greenwood, Sadja, M.D. *Menopause Naturally: Preparing for the Second Half of Life.* Volcano, Calif.: Volcano Press, 1984.

Greer, Germaine. *The Change: Women, Aging, and the Menopause.* New York: Fawcett Columbine, 1991.

Halprin, Sara. *"Look at My Ugly Face": Myths and Musings on Beauty and Other Perilous Obsessions With Women's Appearance.* New York: Viking, 1995.

Hillman, James. *The Soul's Code: In Search of Character and Calling.* New York: Random House, 1994.

Horrigan, Bonnie J. *Red Moon Passage: The Power and Wisdom of Menopause.* New York: Crown Publishers, 1996.

Jacobowitz, Ruth S. *150 Most-Asked Questions About Menopause: What Women Really Want to Know.* New York: Hearst Books, 1993.

Jones, James W. *In the Middle of This Road We Call Our Life: The Courage to Search for Something More.* New York: HarperCollins, 1995.

Jung, Carl G. *The Portable Jung.* Edited by Joseph Campbell. New York: The Viking Press, 1971.

Kelly, G. Lombard, M.D. *A Doctor Discusses Menopause.* Chicago: Budlong Press, 1967.

Kohn, Alfie. *No Contest: The Case Against Competition.* New York: Houghton Mifflin, 1986.

Laux, Marcus, N.D., and Christine Conrad. *Natural Woman, Natural Menopause.* New York: HarperCollins, 1997.

Lee, John R., M.D., with Virginia Hopkins. *What Your Doctor May Not Tell You About Menopause: The Breakthrough Book on Natural Progesterone.* New York: Warner Books, 1996.

Levinson, Daniel J. *The Seasons of a Man's Life.* New York: Ballantine, 1978.

Love, Susan, M.D., with Karen Lindsey. *Dr. Susan Love's Hormone Book: Making Informed Choices About Menopause.* New York: Random House, 1997.

Maslow, Abraham H. *The Farther Reaches of Human Nature*. New York: Viking Penguin, 1971.

———. *Toward a Psychology of Being*. New York: Van Nostrand Reinhold, 1968.

Menopause: A Midlife Passage. Edited by Joan C. Callahan. Indianapolis: Indiana University Press, 1993.

Nachtigall, Lila, M.D., and Joan Rattner Heilman. *Estrogen: A Complete Guide to Reversing the Effects of Menopause Using Hormone Replacement Therapy*. New York: HarperCollins, 1991.

O'Brien, Mary E., M.D. *In Sickness and in Health: What Every Man Should Know About the Woman He Loves*. Santa Fe, N.M.: Health Press, 1991.

Page, Susan. *Now That I'm Married, Why Isn't Everything Perfect? The Eight Essential Traits of Couples Who Thrive*. Boston: Little Brown, 1994.

Peck, M. Scott, M.D. *The Road Less Traveled: A New Psychology of Love, Traditional Values and Spiritual Growth*. New York: Simon and Schuster, 1978.

Perry, Susan, and Katherine A. O'Hanlan, M.D. *Natural Menopause: The Complete Guide to a Woman's Most Misunderstood Passage*. Reading, Mass.: Addison Wesley, 1992.

Ross, Pat. *Menopause Madness: An Empathetic Little Book*. New York: Simon and Schuster, 1998.

Sacks, Martha. *Menopaws: The Silent Meow*. Berkeley, Calif.: Ten Speed Press, 1995.

Sand, Gayle. *Is It Hot in Here or Is It Me?: A Personal Look at the Facts, Fallacies, and Feelings of Menopause*. New York: HarperCollins, 1993.

Schlessinger, Dr. Laura C. *Ten Stupid Things Men Do to Mess Up Their Lives*. New York: HarperCollins, 1997.

Seaman, Barbara, and Gideon Seaman, M.D. *Women and the Crisis in Sex Hormones*. New York: Bantam Books, 1977.

Selye, Hans, M.D. *Stress Without Distress*. New York: J. B. Lippincott, 1974.

———. *The Stress of Life*. New York: McGraw Hill, 1956.

Sheehy, Gail. *New Passages: Mapping Your Life Across Time*. New York: Random House, 1995.

———. *The Silent Passage: Menopause*. New York: Random House, 1991.

———. *Understanding Men's Passages: Discovering the New Map of Men's Lives*. New York: Random House, 1998.

Tannen, Deborah, Ph.D. *You Just Don't Understand: Women and Men in Conversation*. New York: Ballantine Books, 1990.

Thomas, Lewis. *The Lives of a Cell*. New York: The Viking Press, 1974.

Utian, Wulf H., M.D., Ph.D., and Ruth S. Jacobowitz. *Managing Your Menopause*. New York: Simon and Schuster, 1990.

Weed, Susun S. *Menopausal Years: The Wise Woman Way*. Woodstock, N.Y.: Ash Tree Publishing, 1992.

Wells, Robert G., M.D., and Mary C. Wells. *Menopause and Midlife*. Wheaton, Ill.: Living Books, 1990.

West, Stanley, M.D., with Paula Dranov. *The Hysterectomy Hoax*. New York: Doubleday, 1994.

When I Am an Old Woman I Shall Wear Purple. Edited by Sandra Haldeman Martz. Watsonville, Calif.: Papier-Mache Press, 1987.

Whyte, David. *The Heart Aroused: Poetry and the Preservation of the Soul in Corporate America*. New York: Doubleday, 1994.

Wilson, Robert A., M.D. *Feminine Forever*. New York: M. Evans and Company, 1966.

Women of the 14th Moon: Writings on Menopause. Edited by Dena Taylor and Amber Coverdale Sumrall. Freedom, Calif.: The Crossing Press, 1991.

Wright, Jonathan V., M.D., and John Morgenthaler. *Natural Hormone Replacement for Women Over 45*. Petaluma, Calif.: Smart Publications, 1997.

*A*cknowledgments

I must start by thanking my wife, Susan, for being willing to have her private life talked about in public. Throughout her menopause, she has been an inspirational example of strength and wisdom. She's also been a patient editor and a tremendous support system. Thanks, Sus'.

I also thank my children, Erin and Matthew. Erin is the best natural editor I've ever known. I deeply appreciate the way she was able to call me up short when I was way off base, yet still let me know she thinks I'm okay. Matthew has that intuitive ability to have always been there with enthusiasm just when I needed it. Thanks for believing in the project, you two.

Appreciation goes to my two brothers-in-law, John Sasser and John Burgess, who were kind enough to suffer through a terrible early draft. Their comments have made this a far better book. Thanks also to their supportive wives: my sister, Nancy, and Susan's sister, Lin.

Special thanks go to three people who have believed in this book for years: Susan Page, Dorothy Wall, and Burton Hersh. Without their support, I would have quit long ago.

I must also offer deep gratitude to four people who combined to make the book's genesis possible: to Jerre Sears for giving us the river trip; to John Campbell for being there in just the right way at the perfect moment; to George Trim for hearing and responding; and to Brugh Joy for enabling us all to be together.

George Trim deserves special mention. He has been an example of patience and strength for me, as well as a support system. He's walked me through this project every step of the way, as a friend, professional, and mentor. There are not many people on the planet who give as unconditionally as George. Thank you, sir.

167

I had no idea how much a book is a team project. I am eternally grateful to Dorothy Wall for her editing, without which this book would have been unreadable. Thanks also go to Sonia Nordenson for her wise fine-tuning, and to Tamsen George for all her behind-the-scenes help. Pam Farmer, M.D., Jonathan V. Wright, M.D., Bill Affolter, M.D., Bradley Bongiovanni, N.D., Uli Kanoor, N.D., and Katherine Martin, D.O., were very helpful with professional advice and suggestions.

Finally, thanks to Michael and Chris Adcock for their help, love, and support.

Index

169

Other outstanding relationship books

Dancing in the Dark
The Shadow Side of Intimate Relationships
Douglas & Naomi Moseley

"A + √ [TOP RATING]. This book is not for the faint-hearted, but it is for those who want to take their relationship to a glorious level—and are willing to do the work in the shadows to get there."
Marriage Magazine

"Bravo! Brava! Finally a book with real solutions for real relationships . . . a must-read for individuals, couples, and helping professionals."
Pat Love, Ed.D., co-author, *Hot Monogamy*

Fishing by Moonlight
The Art of Choosing Intimate Partners
Colene Sawyer, Ph.D.

Winner: 1997 Clark Vincent Award from the California Association of Marriage and Family Therapists

"From healing past pain to preparing for a healthy mate, this book is filled with useful insights."
John Gray, Ph.D., author, *Men Are From Mars, Women Are From Venus*

Riding the Dragon
The Power of Committed Relationship
Rhea Powers & Gawain Bantle

"A radically fresh, challenging, and inspired path into vastly expanded personal and mutual development attainable through a committed relationship."
W. Brugh Joy, M.D., author, *Joy's Way* and *Avalanche*

"A wise, bold, honest map through the maze of intimate relationship. Rhea and Gawain are delightful mirrors, reflecting hope, courage, and inspiration for all lovers."
Gabrielle Roth, author, *Maps to Ecstasy: Teachings of an Urban Shaman*

Other outstanding transition books

The Sound of the Earth
A Man's Mid-Life Passage and Spiritual Awakening
Hart Sprager

"Hart Sprager has given us a heartfelt and enthralling account of the spritual path. This is a book to be savored, page by page. Enjoy!"
Michael Toms
Co-founder, New Dimensions Radio
Author, *At the Leading Edge*

". . . mesmerizing honesty . . . exquisite sensitivity, *The Sound of the Earth* conveys a distinct impression . . . that we are being guided into a new and initially strange land of awakened sprituality."
Science of Mind **magazine**

Strings: The Miracle of Life
John B. Robbins

"Robbins brilliantly details the incredible complex, miraculous, and intricate world of medicine . . . a roller coaster of suspense that the reader will find difficult to put down . . . will both inspire readers and deepen their spirituality. Highly recommended."
Foreword **Magazine**

". . . incredible page-turning account . . . Around this true medical thriller is woven a wonderfully articulate description of Robbin's own Buddhist perspectives, and the wrestling he does with the contradictions, paradoxes, and ironies of American medicine and of life itself."
NAPRA ReView

Spirituality
Where Body and Soul Encounter the Sacred
Carl McColman

"Spirituality provides multiple doorways of comfort and insight . . . a practical book for personal, professional, and deep interior exploration."
Angeles Arrien, Ph.D., Cultural Anthropologist, author,
The Four-Fold Way **and** *Signs of Life*

"Carl McColman writes from within a clear religious tradition, but in a way which is open and accessible to people who are struggling with what they con believe. His book will be of great help to many people."
Kenneth Leech, author, *Soul Friend* **and** *True Prayer*

Public Library of New London
New London, CT 06320

A2130 145348 5

FINES 10¢ PER DAY